# OVER MY DEAD BODY!

Excerpts from the Book

*The Story of Hillside Cemetery*
*1873 - 1988*

*Silverton*
*San Juan County*
*Colorado*

**Freda Carley Peterson**

Library of Congress Catalog Card No. 96-76377

ISBN 0-927562-20-0

Printed in the United States of America

Cover Design by Bill Cason

Need extra copies of **OVER MY DEAD BODY** for a friend
or your local library?
Send $11.95 per book plus $2.00 postage and handling
for the first copy; add $1.00 postage for each additional copy.

Published by

freda28@juno.com
Freda Peterson Gooch
804 Empire, Box 610
Silverton, CO 81433

# PROLOGUE

*In serene repose on Boulder's breast*
*Age and youth lie in peaceful rest.*
*This mountain has in trust to hold*
*A dust more precious than dust of gold*
*by A.L. Maxwell*
*former Silverton resident and historian*

High in the rugged San Juan Range of the Rocky
Mountains in Southwestern Colorado lies the little
town of Silverton. Originally an isolated mining
camp, it is now known worldwide as the destination of
the narrow gauge passenger train which originates in
Durango. Silverton was settled in the early 1870s and
is the only town in San Juan County still in existence.
Animas Forks, Chattanooga, Eureka, Gladstone,
Howardsville, Mineral Point and Red Mountain Town,
former nearby towns, did not survive.

Hillside Cemetery is sprawled over the lower slope of
Boulder Mountain within sight of town. Make your
way north up the main street (Greene) past the court
house, and over the bridge. Boulder Mountain is in
front of you. Although 3,050 burials have been
documented, only one-third that number are marked
with tombstones or temporary markers. Many graves
were identified at one time with wooden markers or
rocks, but the harsh winters and years have taken
their toll. Very few of those graves can be identified
today. When summer comes, decorating the cemetery
with daisies and wildflowers, the long destructive
winter is forgotten for a time. It's a pleasure to
introduce you to a few of the men, women, children
and innocent babes who now rest forever at Hillside.

# HILLSIDE CEMETERY
## SECTOR IDENTIFICATION PLAT

There is no official record of burial locations in Hillside Cemetery. This plat uses a system of sector numbers to help locate a particular grave. **Each entry for a burial with a known location is identified in this book by a sector number in parentheses below the name of the individual.** That sector number correlates to the numbered sector on the plat. Tombstones which can be seen from the road and which mark the general area of the various sectors are:

(1) Flu Marker, Harrison
(2) Molinario, Casagranda
(3) Thompson, Bastian
(4) Cole, Brown
(5) Todeschi, Sutherland
(6) Steadman, Eaker, Grey
(7) Sleep, McLeod
(8) Smith, Pearson
(9) Grisenti, Johnson
(10) Sims
(11) Beckman, Mason
(12) Giono, Caine
(13) Stinson, Sullivan, Hunt

(14) Mulford, Snider
(15) Giacomelli, Berkey
(16) Salazar, Scherer
(17) Weed
(18) Hilton
(19) Bertram, Fahrion
(20) Sauser, Weir
(21) Dresback
(22) Bryan, Brown
(23) Miller, Brammeier
(24) Nelson, Payne
(25) Castleton, Short

....................................................................

*The packer's shout, with which these gulches rang,*
*Is stilled forever. And no men abide*
*In those log cabins crumbling into dust.*
*They loved this land, those men who went before ...*
*Those giants lived in grandeur here, serene.*
*Today their trail is dim, almost unseen.*
*Patrick Fancher*

# HILLSIDE CEMETERY
## SECTOR IDENTIFICATION PLAT

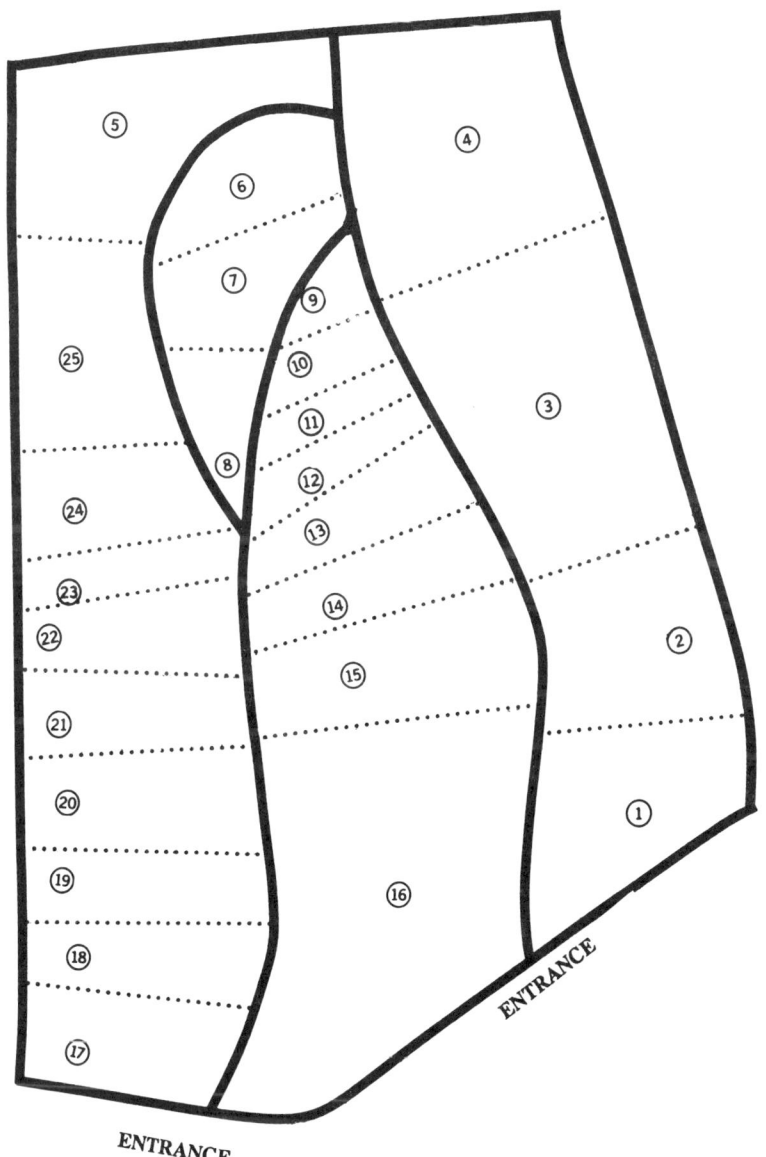

*The Story of Hillside Cemetery* in its unabridged form
contains entries for more than 3,000 burials, as well as
many additional details (names, dates, places, events)
of genealogical interest to family researchers.

For information on the unabridged version of the book
*The Story of Hillside Cemetery*, contact:

**Freda Carley Peterson**
**c/o San Juan County Historical Society**
**Box 154, Silverton, CO 81433**

## ABBOTT, GEORGE C. - Snowslide

No Marker - 1856 - Mar 17, 1906 - Age 50 Years - George and his partner in the Bonner Mine, "Lucky Bill" Thompson, went to their deaths in the great storm. George Strayer and his brother operated claims across the gulch from the Bonner Mine, and they made it in to town Monday afternoon to report that late Saturday night a gigantic slide crashed down the mountainside and left no vestige of the Bonner property, George Abbott or "Lucky Bill" Thompson. On that same day a total of 18 men in the county met death in a rash of snowslides.

Abbott and Thompson were working the Bonner on a contract; there were three cabins which had been built on the property about ten years previously, and all were considered safe from snowslides. The slide which killed the men started at the edge of the green timber 400 feet above the cabins and plowed its way through a patch of dry timber. In its descent it passed over two of the cabins without harming them, then struck the cabin where Abbott and Thompson had retired for the night, took off the roof and logs on one side, packed the building with snow, and ended at the bottom of the gulch some 300 feet below.

A rescue party, organized in Silverton, slowly made their way through the snow to the scene of the tragedy, about seven miles from Silverton up Mineral Creek. The next afternoon, Tuesday, they found Abbott's body and brought it to town the next day. He was found in his bunk, crushed under the weight of the logs of the cabin which had fallen on his head and body. He was evidently asleep when death came, and the clock at the head of the bed stopped at the hour of 11:00, an hour significant of death with the Order of Elks, to which his partner, Thompson, belonged. "Lucky Bill" was not found until May 31st, more than two months later, buried under three feet of snow and ice in the cabin.

George Abbott, born in Texas, never married. A man of quiet, gentlemanly demeanor, he was well liked and respected in the community. The family moved to Colorado in 1880 and located at Silver Plume then moved to the Silverton area in 1884. He had always worked at mining. For a few years when the Neglected Mine, near Durango, was proving to be a great gold producer, George held the position as foreman of that mine, and when the property closed down he returned to Silverton and formed a partnership with "Lucky Bill" Thompson. George was considered a first class miner and had many friends in and around Silverton. About two months before he and "Lucky Bill" were killed, they had made their way from the Bonner Mine to Silverton through deep snow and across five snowslides, some of them very large. It took them five hours to traverse the snow to town, where they took a couple of days of rest.

George's funeral was held at Miners Union Hall at 2:30 in the afternoon under the auspices of the Fraternal Order of Eagles. After the impressive and beautiful burial service of the Eagles, Rev. Charles Mohr of the Congregational Church delivered the funeral sermon. About 15 members of the Eagles followed the remains to their last resting place at Hillside Cemetery, headed by the Eagles Brass Band. Burial was perhaps beside his parents; however there are no markers for the Abbott family.

George Boss, who operated the livery, feed and stage stable at 1322 Blair Street, submitted a bill for George Abbott's funeral to the Fraternal Order of Eagles. The itemized invoice listed two teams and drivers $12.00; printing $1.50; telephone 50 cents; band $35.00; preacher $5.00; and Prosser Undertaking $107.50. The bill for $107.50

from Laura G. Prosser, Undertaker and Furniture Dealer (carpets, linoleums, blankets and window shades) was itemized to include one casket $75.00; robe $5.00; fluid and services $5.00; grave $10.00; teams for casket and preacher $9.00; express on box 50 cents; flowers $3.00.

## ALEXANDER, FRANK
No Marker - Died Sept 14, 1887 - Age 40 Years - Frank, a pioneer of the Eureka mining district, died at the residence of Eugene McCarthy after being suddenly taken ill with pneumonia. A native of Silesia Province in Prussia, he came to America in about 1865, and had been in the San Juan since 1875. His funeral at the Knights of Labor Hall was attended by a large concourse of friends, and burial was at a Hillside. Frank's partner and very best friend, Maurice Condon, was so affected by Frank's death that he took to heavy drinking; about five weeks after Frank's death, Maurice, who had been a splendid physical specimen, died on a billiard table in the Star of the West Saloon.

## ALLHOFF, BEN - Died in a Privy
No Marker - Died Sept 19, 1901 - On a Thursday afternoon at about 2:00 o'clock, Ben, who had been sick two weeks, was lying in the

sun on the west side of the Trembath Boarding House and appeared to be suffering untold agony with stomach complaint. Shortly after saying he did not want to be moved to his room, he was discovered to be missing. About an hour later he was found in the outhouse where he had fallen head first into the vault.

Ben was about 35 years old and had worked as a helper at the Kendrick-Gelder Smelter. Burial took place from the undertaker's the next day. No other information was found.

**ANDERSON, JOE** - Flu Epidemic
(4) - Oct 16, 1888 - Oct 31,1918 - Age 30 Years - At the height of the flu epidemic in Silverton, Joe died at Miners Union Hospital just two days after the death of his wife, Christina. Almost ten percent of Silverton's population died within a three week period. A well known mining man, Joe had been in mining partnerships with Nels Andrene and Ernest Jackson. Both those men also died in the devastating epidemic ... Nels on October 29th, Ernest on the same day as Joe's death. They are also buried at Hillside.

Joe was born at Kulmar, Sweden, and had lived in the Silverton area about seven years. He and Miss Christina Anderson were married at the court house in Silverton by Judge Palmquist on May 31, 1916; their friends, Hulda Backman and Edward Johnson, were also married at that happy time. During the worldwide flu epidemic a couple of years later, all four were stricken with the disease and only Hulda Backman Johnson survived.

**ANDERSON, ROBERT** - Shot
No Marker - Died July 29, 1880 - On a Thursday evening at about 7:00, while Doc Grow was "taking his tea", he was suddenly summoned over to his slaughterhouse by his partner, Mr. Mayer. Upon arriving there, he found one of his employees, Charles Siegel, who helped him do his slaughtering, in a state of great excitement. Siegel, gesticulating wildly, was utterly unable to articulate anything comprehensible. After quieting him somewhat, Doc succeeded in learning Siegel had accidentally shot a young man by the name of Robert Anderson at Gus Ambold's nearby slaughterhouse.

Siegel had been preparing to butcher a steer and as was the custom, proceeded to shoot the animal before dressing it. He aimed and fired, but the steer did not drop, and he supposed the bullet had misfired. He put another cartridge in the gun, recapped it and took aim to fire again, when suddenly the steer dropped. Siegel put the gun down without firing it and proceeded to dress the steer. After finishing the job, he put the gun under his right arm and walked over to the Ambold slaughterhouse to see how they were getting on with their butchering. He stood in the door joking with the boys and, making a motion with his arm, accidentally discharged the gun. The ball grazed the stomach of one of the workmen and hit young Robert Anderson, sitting on the other side of the slaughterhouse, killing him almost instantly.

Dr. Robert H. Brown arrived and found the body already getting cold. It was evident from an informal viewing of the body that Anderson's neck was broken and the ball had passed through his heart. A jury consisting of John Ufford, Charles Bayles, E. Homann, George Swan, F. M. Snowden and H.O. Wing, was empaneled. Coroner Ballou and other officers repaired to the slaughterhouse where a preliminary examination took place. Several witnesses were questioned, and also Siegel, the unfortunate man who did the shooting. After a careful consideration of the sad case by the jury, they rendered a verdict that Robert Anderson came to his death by a gun accidentally discharged in the hands of

Charles Siegel. While this was a sad commentary upon carelessness in handling firearms, it was felt the jury did their duty in entirely exonerating Siegel. There was not the slightest evidence of any ill feeling between the men or between the two slaughterhouse gangs. Siegel had no acquaintance with the deceased and had not spoken ten words to him in his life.

Robert Anderson, the victim, was a resident of Ft. Collins, Laramie County, Colorado, had been in Silverton only about two weeks, and employed at Ambold's slaughterhouse about nine days. He was buried on a Friday at the Silverton cemetery with Rev. H.P. Roberts officiating.

## ASHLEY, INFANT TWIN GIRL
No Marker - Apr 11, 1905 - This little girl, daughter of Edward J. and Agnes Freeman Ashley, was stillborn at the family home in Howardsville and was buried at Hillside the next day. A sister of this child, Mary Elizabeth Ashley, had died about a year previously.

Ted Ashley, twin brother of this little girl, went to school in Ouray and spent much of his life there and in California. He retired from his engineering career in 1965, and in July 1973 visited Howardsville, his birthplace. During that visit he was stricken with a heart attack and died about 30 feet from the place where he was born. Ted was buried in the Ouray Cemetery; his survivors included his wife, Eva Ruth, two children and several grandchildren.

**ATTERBURY, WALTER** - Suicide after Holdup
No Marker - Died Oct 1, 1904 - A little before 1:00 a.m. on the first day of October, Walter, dressed in blue overalls and jumper and large black hat and black mask, burst through the front door of the Hub Saloon in the Grand Hotel. Brandishing two fierce looking long-barreled weapons, he gave the command "All hands up!" to the nine or ten people in the place. Herman Stroble, manager of the saloon, was standing in front of the bar talking to three men, one of whom was John Loftus; Stroble quickly turned and grappled with the robber, at the same time calling for help. The masked man started shooting, and one bullet struck the bar, glanced upward and struck Jimmie Bothwell, the barkeeper, in the shoulder. That bullet went on through Bothwell and hit the ice chest.

Another shot hit John Loftus at close range in the abdomen. He sank to the floor mortally wounded, and died within a few minutes. His only words were "My God, I'm done for!"

Joe "Shorty" Wagner, an employee of the house, tried to help Stroble and got behind the robber. But the robber was too quick, and turned around and took a shot at Shorty. That shot went past Shorty's head and through the window. Shorty went on out the front door.

Then Walter, the holdup man, slammed Stroble over the head and shot him twice, one bullet striking him in the right side, being deflected by a rib, and the other going through the fleshy part of his leg. It was later determined a nerve had been severed, which caused Stroble many problems the rest of his life.

When Stroble dropped to the floor, wounded and exhausted, Walter went to the back door, still keeping a gun trained on the crowd. The back door was locked so he went into the water closet, broke out a window and jumped through, cutting his face and hands severely.

Walter's exit through the window did not end the tragedy. Sheriff Casad instituted a search, and at about 7:00 a.m. the next morning found him lying dead in an alley between Reese and Snowden, 13th and 14th Streets. He had placed the muzzle of his six-shooter in his mouth, pulled the trigger and sent a bullet through his brain, literally tearing off the back of his head. The body was taken to the undertaking rooms and searched, but no clues were found as to the desperate man's identity, and no one recognized him, although some remembered seeing him around camp. Around his neck was fastened a large sack, where he had planned to place the money from the holdup, and in his pockets were four silver dollars. He was described as six feet tall, about 160 pounds, 28 to 30 years old, smooth shaven, with brown hair and blue eyes, large nose and chin, and was presumed to be of foreign birth. Hundreds of residents of Silverton and the adjacent mining camps came to view the distorted body as it lay in the morgue, alongside the dead victim of the tragedy, John Loftus. None could identify the man until George Fessenden, a Eureka saloon keeper, came into the undertaking rooms and at a single glance announced the body to be that of Walter Atterbury, who had worked for him.

Atterbury's actions were simply incomprehensible to all who knew him. He was a favorite and friend of all who knew him, honest in all transactions and a hard worker. There was a rumor that for some months he had been closely associated with a certain Eureka gambler (not named), and his downfall dated from the beginning of that association. Friends of Walter contributed the necessary money to pay for his funeral, which was held on a Monday afternoon, concluding at Hillside Cemetery.

**AVI, LOUIS** - Snowslide
(2) - June 27, 1873 - Feb 17, 1900 - Age 26 Years - His grave is marked by a tall gray stone, fenced, near the Sartore plot.

Near the Sampson Mine on Bonita Mountain, Louis Avi, George Foster, Ed McKay and Tony Tam were plodding through snow on the mountain trail on their way to Silverton to attend the funeral of their friend, John D. Lewis. Lewis had been killed in a snowslide the day before. Little did the men dream the same fate could be awaiting them.

Avi and Foster, 20 feet ahead of the others on the trail, were doomed when a slide broke loose from above, engulfed them, and almost instantly faded them from sight down the incline of death; other slides followed from right to left, and everything grew dizzy under the whirl of snow which boiled, bubbled and seethed like a cauldron. The entire mountain seemed to be moving downward, while the bubbling snow appeared to move slowly. The first slide, with its victims, plunged over a cliff and into the gulch a thousand feet below; then the other slides spread over it. The entire affair was over in 30 seconds from the first break of the snow. Erick Sutherland, who was riding the tram at the time, saw the men pitched like corks on the billowy mass until the second slide covered them. Snow was piled 40 to 60 feet deep in the gulch.

The Gold King Mine force immediately started digging for the missing men. Foster's body was found the next morning and the remains were taken to Durango for burial, accompanied by his father, brother, and heart-broken bride of one month, the former Mary Lechner. George was 24 years old. (Mary died in Durango in 1945 and is buried at Greenmount Cemetery.)

Louis Avi's body could not be found, although the search continued for two weeks. About four months later, in May, the two Avi brothers and three cousins continued the search and dug a hole into the middle of the slide so the water could run through the slide; about a week later they cut a tunnel above the water course. In early June they found Louis' hat and other clothing during a tunnel search in deep snow, and finally, after three weeks of hard labor by seven men constantly at work digging a tunnel more than 600 feet long in the snow, Louis Avi's body was found. The men, in addition to digging, attached a hose from a stream of water on the mountainside to use as a hydraulic to remove the huge banks of snow, and by this process at last located the remains of Louis Avi. He was found by his brother, John Avi, and Joe Vetter. The body was brought to Silverton on the evening train from Gladstone, accompanied by his brothers John and Mike, and his cousin, Frank Avi.

Louis, born in Tirol, Pine, Austria, where his father still lived, had lived in Silverton about six years, and had worked at the Gold King Mine the last two years. Survivors in the area were his brothers, John and Mike Avi, and his cousin, Frank Avi, as well as a host of friends. His funeral was held at Miners Union Hall, on a Sunday afternoon with Colonel Barney O'Driscoll preaching the sermon. After the service, fully 75 miners, members of the Miners Union, headed by the San Juan Brass Band, formed the funeral procession which slowly marched to Hillside Cemetery for the burial.

Louis' brothers, John and Mike Avi, spent a week in October of 1900 beautifying the grave of their brother at Hillside Cemetery. They enclosed the grave with a neat fence and placed a marble monument so their loved one would be remembered.

Mike Avi, brother of Louis and John F., died of typhoid May 18, 1903, in Denver, Colorado. He was about 41 years old, learned to become an expert miner in Westphalia, Prussia, and traveled in South America. His survivors included his father and a brother in Tyrol and a brother in Denver. Michael had moved from Silverton to Denver about seven months before his death.

**BACKMAN, ERICK JOHN** - Snowslide (11) - Jan 26, 1860 - Mar 6, 1919 - Age 59 - The family name "Backman" was sometimes spelled "Beckman".

The deadly snowslide caught John below what was known as the break-over on the Iowa-Tiger tram, near the Iowa Mill in Arrastra Gulch. He had been in town visiting his family, and was on his way back to his job as tram man at the Iowa Mill. He seated himself in a tram bucket to ride the aerial tram across the canyon to the mill. For some reason the tram stalled, and John became bitterly cold swinging in the bucket suspended over the canyon. He decided to climb out of the bucket, then, hanging suspended over the canyon, carefully made his way hand over hand along the cable to a tram tower, climbed down to the ground, then started to walk the rest of the way up to the mill. It was about 10:30 a.m. John had barely reached the ground when it happened ... the huge avalanche came down with a rush, completely inundating and sweeping him away. His body was found by mine employees at about 2:00 that Thursday afternoon.

John was born in Varmland, Sweden, came to America in about 1909 and to Silverton in 1911, where other family members later joined him. He was well thought of in the area, had a cheerful disposition and always looked at the bright side of life. Survivors were his wife, Maria (Mary) Johnson Backman, whom he had married in Sweden in 1885; daughters, Amanda, Hulda, Esther, Agnes and Svea, and sons, Elmer, Fritz and Ragnar. John was buried at Hillside where other family members were later laid to rest near him.

## BAILEY, MARY ELIZABETH

No Marker - Dec 23, 1905 - Dec 31, 1905 - Age 8 days - In announcing this baby's birth, the newspaper noted that Jack Bailey, the assayer, had taken a few days off to celebrate the occasion of a new little girl at his house. The baby's maternal grandmother made preparations to come to Silverton from Elgin, Illinois, but arrived the day after the baby died of inflammatory degeneration of the liver after being ill a week. Dr. Fox tended the sick child. Her father was born in Dallas, Texas, and her mother, the former Jennie Hoagland, was born in Elgin, Illinois. Mary Elizabeth was buried at Hillside January 3, 1906.

*"Another little darling babe*
*is sheltered in the grave.*
*God needed one more angel child*
*amidst his shining band,*
*and so he bent with loving smile*
*and clasped our darling's hand."*

## BAILEY, SANDY - Died Shoveling Snow

No Marker - Died Feb 24, 1884 (approximately) - While shoveling snow off the railroad track near Elk Park, Sandy suddenly collapsed and died from exhaustion. A crude coffin was constructed by his fellow workmen, Sandy was carefully laid out in it, then buried in the snow to await the time when the train could again get through the heavy snow to Silverton. Bailey was an old timer of the San Juan, and had been in the region about ten years, but hardly anything was known of his background. He and several other men had been laboring daily for about two weeks attempting to shovel the enormous snowslides from the railroad tracks. The slides, full of timber and trees up to two feet in diameter, also had boulders weighing tons scattered throughout. The entire mass was a solid block of ice. Men like Sandy, who shoveled snowslides from the railroad track, worked for a dollar a day.

The winter of 1883-1884 was a particularly deadly one in the San Juan. The deep snow paralyzed transportation, and there were no trains arriving in Silverton from February 2nd until April 10th. There was such a terrible loss of life from avalanches in the Silverton, Ouray and Telluride districts, it was never accurately determined exactly how many died that winter.

**BALDESSARI, LUCIA** - Picture on Marker (23) - Dec 25, 1872 - Oct 9, 1902 - Her tombstone reads "1863-1902", but is believed to be in error.

Lucia, who was born in Val Filoriana, Tyrol, Austria, and came to the U.S. in 1899, met with a frightful and fatal accident on a late Thursday afternoon. As Charles H. Bertram, the dairyman, was driving up Blair Street seated on his wagon loaded high with baled hay, Lucia stopped him to hand some meat up to him. During the conversation she climbed up on the brake of the wagon and grasped the rope binding the load. Suddenly, the horses bolted and tore down the street, with Lucia hanging on to the rope for dear life. The horses raced around the corner into 14th Street, and in front of Squire Watson's residence the load of hay shifted then crashed off the wagon and landed on top of the unfortunate woman. She was carried to her home and medical aid summoned, but her injuries were fatal. She had broken ribs, crushed lungs and other internal injuries, complicated by the fact that she was about to be "confined" (give birth). She lived in great agony about 30 minutes, then died, along with her unborn child.

Survivors were her husband, Giorgio, who worked at the Sunnyside Mine, and her little two year old boy. Her funeral was held on a Saturday afternoon, with burial taking place at Hillside. Lucia's husband, Giorgio, died in

1917 and is also buried at Hillside; no further information was found regarding their son, who was two years old when his mother died.

## BARNETT, WILLIAM

No Marker - 1873 - Nov 12, 1916 - Age 43 Years - William's body was found by an employee of the Western Colorado Power Company on November 13, 1916, lying on the ground about a quarter of a mile above the old Rose Smelter. Death was due to exposure by exposure, freezing and miners con, from which he had suffered five years. He had been working at the Galty Boy Mine near Gladstone, but had to stop working because of feeling ill. He apparently was walking toward town when he had a coughing attack, fell and couldn't get up, then had a hemorrhage. Overcome by the frigid temperatures and the ravages of the disease, he died.

Born in Redruth, Cornwall, England, he had been in the Silverton area about 14 years, and in Colorado 25 years. In 1908 he was married at Ophir, Colorado, to a woman whose name was not found. The couple had a son whom he adored, and when his wife's health forced her to return to England with their little son, he grieved many months over the loss of their companionship. During his lifetime, he was a faithful father and kind husband. The funeral for William was held at McLeod Undertaking Parlor and many of his old friends attended. He was buried at Hillside, perhaps near his brother, Richard, who died the previous February.

**BARRY, FRED R.** - Exposure and Freezing No Marker - Oct 19, 1853 - Dec 29, 1910 (approximately) - Age 57 Years - The exact date of Fred's death would never be known, as he died alone on a mountain. He was an old time prospector and trapper who had not been seen since December 29th when he left Silverton in the deep snow to return to his cabin in the Bear Creek district, about sixteen miles from Silverton, near the Continental Divide, where he owned and worked the Hercules group of claims in that district.

When he didn't show up at his cabin in a reasonable length of time, Dave McPhillips, who lived in the same area, came to Silverton in search of him. He and Patrick J. McDermott then returned to Bear Creek, making a careful search for Fred on the way. They didn't find him and the opinion was generally accepted that he had been caught in one of the numerous slides that had run along the route he would have followed.

After McDermott returned to Silverton, Dave McPhillips kept looking for Fred, and finally, on January 11th, found his remains lying in the snow on the trail a few hundred feet from his cabin. It appeared he had reached his cabin, had later gone outside and died. McPhillips covered the body with snow and again made the long and arduous trip to Silverton to get help. Coroner R.E. McLeod selected a jury composed of Al Marshall, Johnson Morehead, Ludwig Vota, Angelo Vota, Mike Coughlin, Horace Henry and Dave McPhillips. These men accompanied the coroner back to Bear Creek to transport the remains back to Silverton. In the middle of winter in the high mountains, the trip was a hard and dangerous one and would take at least four days. When they reached Bear Creek and Fred's body, the men determined Fred Barry died of exposure and freezing.

Ring, Fred's dog and constant companion, was with him when death came and had tramped back and forth from the cabin door to the body of his dead master for eleven days and nights, forming an icy path. The dog remained faithful and true, watching as a guard over the body, and had apparently gone eleven days without food. One of the dead man's hands was considerably scratched where his devoted dog had tried to rouse his master. Such is the devotion of dog to man.

Fred had lived in the San Juan over thirty years, and for the last seven years had spent most of his time over in the Bear Creek country working on his Hercules group of claims. He was widely known among the mining men in Colorado and his untimely death was mourned by all. His only known relative was a married sister living in Chicago, Illinois, Mrs. Annie Creedon. Fred was buried at Hillside in a now unmarked grave. Billy Cole, Silverton's pioneer merchant, adopted Fred's faithful dog, Ring.

Dave McPhillips, the friend who found Fred's body, died a couple of years later, in 1913; he also died alone on a mountain in the Bear Creek district. Patrick John McDermott, who also searched for Fred's body, died of pneumonia in November 1915 when he was about 65 years of age. He was described as a sturdy old time prospector who had also worked in the Bear Creek district, born in Ireland, the son of Francis McDermott and Mary Hawley. His body was shipped to a relative, Francis W. McDermott, at Wood River, Nebraska.

## BASARICH, GEORGE - Flu Epidemic

No Marker - Apr 10, 1890 - Oct 27, 1918 - Age 28 Years - George was the 67th person brought to the morgue during the Spanish influenza epidemic which swept Silverton and the world near the end of World War I. Silverton's first death attributed to the flu was on October 18th. George was born in Austria, had lived in the district about six years, and was found dead on Blair Street. He was buried at Hillside October 31, 1918.

## BAUDINO, LUCIA DIGHERA

(3) - Sept 12, 1872 - Mar 23, 1941 - Age 68 Years - Lucia died on an early Sunday morning at the local hospital after a lingering illness. Under the care of Dr. Fred A. Rechnitz several months, she had returned to Silverton the previous Friday from Denver, where she had undergone special treatment. Born at Rivarolo, Canavese, Torino, Italy, Lucia was the daughter of Louis and Virginia Dighera. She immigrated to America in 1906 and married Domenico Baudino, also an Italian immigrant, on Saturday, October 20, 1906, at Leechburg, Armstrong County, Pennsylvania. They made their home in Silverton where Domenico worked in the mines. Children born to them were James (#1) who died in 1907 when a month old, James (#2) in 1910 and

Lena Catarina in 1912 (she later married Louie Dalla). Tragically, as often happened, Lucia's husband, Domenico, was killed in 1913, when he fell 175 feet to his death in the Hamlet Mine, leaving Lucia with a three year old and an eight month old baby. Lucia, in a still strange foreign country, remained in Silverton and worked as a domestic to eke out a living for herself and her two small children. She lived in Silverton more than 30 years, many in the house at 1053 Empire, and left a large circle of friends to mourn her death.

Survivors were her son, James, (married Marjorie Carley), her daughter, Lena (Mrs. Louis Dalla), her nephew and niece, Phil A. Sartore of Silverton and Mary Sartore Vota of Grand Junction. (Phil and Mary were the children of Lucia's sister, Angelina Dighera and Joe Sartore.) Rosary services were held for Lucia at the Maguire Chapel and the funeral was at St. Patrick Catholic Church, Father Lane conducting. Burial was at Hillside beside her husband and little boy. Other family members were later buried near her. Pallbearers were her friends, Snarky Andreatta, Joe Arietta, Henry Bonavida, Dominick Franch, Joe Todeschi and Johnny Troglia.

## BAUSMAN, LAURA VIRGINIA MUSGROVE

(20) - Sept 29, 1859 - Jan 15, 1936 - Age 77 Years - Laura died at the home of her daughter, Adelia (Mrs. James E. Cole), following a paralytic stroke January 4th at her home, 1708 Greene Street. Born in Vicksburg, Mississippi, she was the daughter of Charles and Mrs. Musgrove (often spelled Musgrave). She grew to young womanhood and was educated in Vicksburg, then entered the Cincinnati Conservatory of Music, graduating as an accomplished vocal and instrumental musician. Her musical talent was inherited by several of her twelve children.

Laura was married to George Washington Bausman in St. Louis, Missouri, in January 1883, and their first child, Alexander Musgrove Bausman was born in Vicksburg, Mississippi, in November 1883; at that time George Bausman, the father, was working as desk clerk at the Walker House Hotel in Silverton. Their next three children were born in St. Louis, Missouri: Elizabeth "Bessie" in 1885, George Washington "Rags" in 1887; Adelia Bedorah "Toots" in 1889. Laura's husband divided his time between Silverton and St. Louis, and in May 1890 the entire family moved to Silverton to make their permanent home. The next eight Bausman children were born in Silverton: Caroline "Carrie" in 1891; Joseph Francis in 1892; Laura Virginia "Jinks" in 1893; Helene in 1895, Sallie "Sal" in 1897, Mary Agnes "Mike" in 1899, Frank Isaac "Ike" in 1901, and Marjorie "Nick" in 1903.

In February of 1893 Laura sent for her mother in Vicksburg, Mississippi, to come to Silverton to nurse her back to health; Laura had given birth to her son, Joe, in December 1892, and had been very sick since that time. (Laura didn't have too much time to rest up, as she gave birth to her daughter, "Jinks", the next December.) Laura's mother, whose full name was not found, died in Vicksburg February 3, 1898, at the age of 71 years.

Laura's husband died in January 1903, leaving her with eleven children ranging in age from two to nineteen years, and she was expecting her twelfth child, Marjorie "Nick", who was born three months after her father's death. Although Laura Bausman was artistically talented, she had no business experience and was unable to continue the operation of her husband's mercantile establishment in Silverton. She had a very difficult time raising her large family with practically no means of existence, but she persevered and succeeded. At one point when trying to get her husband's estate settled, she became so frustrated she started for the courthouse with her horsewhip, intending to horsewhip the judge whom she felt was treating her unfairly. As far as is known, she did not carry her intention to fulfillment.

Laura was remembered with affection by those who knew her. If the family had food in the house, they welcomed their friends to eat at their table; if they had no food, they did not let anyone into the house. Laura's children were so artistically and musically talented it was felt several of them could have had successful professional careers in the field of entertainment, if they had so desired. Laura became very hard of hearing and almost blind, but always retained a marvelous sense of humor.

The funeral for Laura was held at her home; pallbearers were her sons-in-law, Charles Pearson, Robert Crawford, Norman Dresback, and her grandsons, Jim W. Cole, Lawrence and Charles Robert Phillips. Burial was in the Bausman family plot at Hillside.

On June 20, 1959, Laura's great-granddaughter, Lois Adelia Cole, was married to James Lee Brown;  On her shoes Lois wore mother of pearl buckles which her great-grandmother, Laura Bausman, had worn on her wedding shoes 77 years previously.

**BAZZANELLA, STEFANIA NONES** - Shot No Marker - Died June 15, 1906 - Age 22 Years - Stella, as she was called in America, was tragically involved in a shooting affray at John Dalla's saloon near the depot (for the train to Gladstone) at about midnight on a summer night in June. Thomas (Tomaso) Franchini was involved in a disturbance in the saloon and was ordered out of the place by Dalla, who backed his words by flourishing a loaded gun.    Threatening to get even, Franchini rushed to his house just north of the saloon, grabbed a shotgun and headed back for the saloon. (The Franchinis and Bazzanellas shared occupancy of the house.)

Stella, who had also been in the saloon, ran after Franchini, intending to stop him, but he burst out of the house with the gun, three shots were fired in rapid succession and Stella, who was halfway between the saloon and the house, fell to the ground, fatally wounded in the left groin.   She died at 6:30 the next morning. There was some question regarding the origin of the gunshots ... it was believed two shots came from a revolver and the other from a shotgun. Ben Bazzanella, Stella's husband, said he saw John Dalla shoot her; others said Dalla fired out the back door to summon authorities. Deputy Sheriff Damschroder arrested and jailed Dalla; Franchini disappeared and a search party was organized to hunt him down.

The parties involved were all Austrians and some of them were with the wounded woman before she died; she told them Franchini shot her. Dr. Fox, who attended her, could not confirm this as Stella did not speak English and he could not understand anything that was said.

Franchini was arrested the next day between Rockwood and Hermosa; he said Dalla had threatened to shoot him so he went to get a shotgun to shoot Dalla. Someone jostled his arm and the gun went off. The newspaper observed that no such disreputable joint as that run by Dalla should be permitted to operate. John Dalla was released from jail and Franchini was locked up. The 22 year old Stella was buried at Hillside June 17, 1906. Stella's father, Thomas Nones, was born in Austria, and her mother, Maria, in Germany. Stella had lived in the Silverton area about two years and she and Ben Bazzanella had been married less than four months; on the previous February 20th in a double wedding ceremony in Silverton, Ben Bazzanella married Stella (Stefania) Nones, and Tomaso Franchini married Maria Biasiori. The event was celebrated by a huge feast and festive ball into the wee hours.

In September 1906 in District Court before Judge Russell, Tomaso Franchini pleaded guilty to the charge of voluntary manslaughter in the killing of Stella. The newspaper noted: "As in all cases where the Austrians are involved, the testimony was conflicting and, as usual, the party got off with a minimum sentence of 14 to 16 months for a woman's life. Voluntary manslaughter and a sentence that really amounts to recreation. Faugh!! The election is close at hand and the Austrian vote is badly needed."

## BECKWITH, ALICE PHULURA
(18) - Temporary Marker - June 23, 1907 - May 17, 1908 - Age 11 Months - On a Sunday night at Oschner hospital in Durango, Alice, the baby girl of Bart (Barzilla) and Ethel Beckwith, was called away from earth by the angel of death. She had suffered intensely from bronchial pneumonia.

Alice, born in Silverton, was the second Beckwith child to die before reaching the age of a year. Fred Carter officiated at Alice's funeral, held in the home of her grandparents in Silverton, William J. and Elizabeth Redda Pearce, and burial was at Hillside Cemetery.

*Somebody's sorrow is making me weep,*
*I know not her name, but echo her cry,*
*for the dearly bought baby*
*she longed so to keep,*
*the baby that rode in its long-lasting sleep*
*in the little white hearse*
*that went rumbling by.*

*I know not her name,*
*but her sorrow I know;*
*while I paused on the crossing*
*I lived it once more,*
*and back to my heart*
*surged that river of woe*
*that but in the breast of a mother can flow,*
*for the little white hearse has been, too,*
*at my door.*
*... Ella Wheeler Wilcox.*

## BEECHER, KATIE LONERGAN

(4) - No Marker - 1874 - May 18, 1902 - Age 28 Years - At St. Joseph Hospital in Denver, Katie died of acute nephritis, the result of an

operation for an "old hurt on the head"; her dying request was that she be buried in Silverton, her former home.

Katie was born in the parish of Ballyhooly, County Cork, Ireland, of old Irish stock, to Paul and Julia Carroll Lonergan. She came to Silverton as a young girl of 16 years in 1890 and, like all Irish girls, came with a chaste heart and a good will. She married Patrick Beecher November 26, 1892, at St. Patrick Catholic Church in Silverton, and they had two children; however the only reference found was for a son born in Silverton January 23, 1897. In 1898, the family moved to Ouray, then to Cripple Creek, where they were living at the time of Katie's death.

Katie's remains arrived in Silverton on Tuesday night and were interred Wednesday afternoon. The funeral service was held at St. Patrick Church, and the text of Rev. Father O'Rourke's sermon, including much poetry, was printed in the newspaper. He noted Katie was a friend to all; cheerful, thoughtful, good natured, and a devout member of the church wherein she was baptized, confirmed, married and wherefrom she was to be buried; she was an earnest and indefatigable worker for the spiritual and temporal welfare of the church to which she belonged; "Katie was pure, spotless and believing, jovial, joyous, not deceiving." She was soon to lie cold in the grave ... "there was the pang!" She was a source of joy to her friends, but all was over now that the faithful heart had ceased to beat. "Ah, there again was the pang!"

Survivors included her husband, Patrick Beecher, and her children (names were not given); her brothers, William Paul "Will the Marshall" Lonergan of Silverton and Maurice P. "Red Mountain Maurice" Lonergan of Red Mountain; her sisters, Bridget Lonergan (Mrs. Edmund) Fox of Silverton and Mrs. Connolly of New York; also her mother and three sisters in Ireland. (Katie's mother, Julia Carroll Lonergan, died April 15, 1912, at Ballyhooly, County Cork, Ireland.) As she had wished, Katie was buried at Hillside; her brother, Maurice P. "Red Mountain Maurice" Lonergan, was later buried near her; his marker is in Sector (4).

Father Cornelius O'Rourke, the priest who presided at Katie's burial and loved poetry, drowned in the Animas River 17 days after Katie's death. He, Mike Coughlin and John McComb were returning to Silverton on horseback from Lake City when the accident occurred. On the bank of the Animas a short distance south of the Tom Moore Mine and about 200 feet from a small wagon bridge which spanned the narrow chasm, the party stopped to adjust Father O'Rourke's saddle. As they were remounting Father O'Rourke's horse veered suddenly, and in so doing struck him a blow which threw the man over the steep cliff. He rolled 40 feet to the swift and turbulent water below. When he saw his friend's peril, brave Jack McComb went to the rescue, but on the steep and slippery bank he too lost his balance, and in less time than it took to tell, both men were struggling in the water. Coughlin scrambled down the bank ahead, but the swift current had swept both men beyond his reach. He climbed back up to the road and ran along the bank to the bridge, then down to the river, hoping to be able to help the men, but neither man was to be seen.

Coughlin went for help, and Rasmus Hansen and Mr. Strong from Eureka came to his aid. The body of McComb was found several hundred yards downstream, having been drawn by the swift current over the dam, under the bridge, then under the snowslide which extended over the river. Father O'Rourke's body was found directly under the bridge, one hand grasping a bridge timber.

Father O'Rourke, born in County Tipperary, Ireland, was 38 years old. At one time he had mined at Leadville, where he and John McComb formed an enduring friendship. The priest, who was extremely popular with the Silverton area people, was buried at Butte, Montana; his friend, John McComb, who went to his death in an effort to save O'Rourke's life, was buried in Denver. Seven years later, in 1909, his daughter, Rowena, was forced to sell her father's properties, including their home, to repay the large debts her father had incurred. She had been a minor child at the time of his death, but had since reached the age to administer his estate.

**BELL, JESSE** - Explosion
No Marker - Died Aug 31, 1893 - On a Saturday morning Jesse, an old timer in the county, was working alone at his mining claim taking giant powder caps out of a box. His pipe dropped off the stool and fell into the box of caps, causing the box to explode instantly. His right hand was blown off at the wrist and several exploding caps went into his stomach.

Suffering greatly, the unfortunate man made several attempts to get into his right hand pants pocket to get his knife so he could put an end to his suffering. Failing in this, he started crawling for Crooke's Mill. "Uncle Tommy" Gifford found him on the road and took the horribly injured man to town. Dr. Pascoe did all that was possible, but the injuries were such that no earthly power could save Jesse. After five days of intense agony, Jesse died on a Thursday morning at 8:30. His body was taken to Prosser's undertaking establishment, prepared for burial and buried the next day in the Silverton cemetery. No survivors were known.

**BENNETT, DOLLIE McCABE** - Snowslide No Marker - 1889 - Jan 5, 1916 - Age 26 Years - Soon after the New Year holidays, Dollie, a pretty petite young woman, and her husband, Harvey, were killed in a gigantic snowslide near the Garry Owen Mine. Harry Castle had been killed two years earlier when the slide ran in the same path.

Dollie and Harvey had come to Silverton a few days earlier with Ed Fiant. Ed had been working a mining property, the Rien Tunnel, but had gone down to Farmington, New Mexico, to spend Christmas with his wife. While he was there, Harvey and Dollie decided to return with him and work at the mine and boarding house. They stayed in Silverton several days to give the slides plenty of time to run, they thought. Harvey had previously come very close to losing his life in the disastrous 1906 St. Patrick's Day snowslide at the Shenandoah Mine when twelve human lives were snuffed out. Nine other men were caught but survived, and Bennett, who was dug out alive, was left with a very real, enduring fear and horror of snowslides.

Ed, Harvey, Dollie and Robert White, who was also returning to the mine with them, decided it was safe enough to proceed to the mine early on a Wednesday morning, and Dollie carried a kitten to keep her company and catch mice at the boarding house. They plodded through the deep snow until they reached the Garry Owen boarding house, where they stopped for dinner, then resumed their journey through the snow. They all crossed the path of the big slide safely, with the exception of Dollie. Near the southeast end of the Sterling Lode, near the Garry Owen Mine, the slide broke with a mighty roar and the great mass of snow came tearing down the mountain toward Dollie. Her horrified husband dashed back into the path of the slide in a frantic effort to save her, but he was too late, and in another second, both were swept 1500 feet down the mountainside to the bottom of Salmhoffer (or Rien) Gulch.

The outer edge of the terrible avalanche engulfed Fiant and White, but did not carry them down with it. When the slide had run, they plunged down the mountain on top of the compacted snow in search of the victims, discovered Bennett's leg protruding from the snow, but were unable to find a trace of Dollie. Because of the eminent danger from a mountain of snow still hanging above the path of the slide, ready to crash down at any moment, it was decided not to endanger more lives, and they abandoned their search.

Harvey's body was extricated from under the snow and taken to Undertaker McLeod's in Silverton. Born in Kansas May 5, 1879, he was the son of D.H. and Anna C. Cook Bennett; his father was born in Michigan, his mother in Illinois. His father, who lived in Colorado Springs, came to Silverton and took his son's body home with him for burial. Harvey was survived by his mother and father, two sisters and a brother.

The search for Dollie's body was discontinued because of another severe storm. When it subsided, between 15 and 25 men worked several days trying to locate her, but the slide was so deep in places the prod poles would not reach the bottom, although the poles were 15 feet long. The men did find Dollie's muff and the kitten she had been carrying.

After the snow began melting in late spring, hardly a day passed that some effort was not made to find Dollie's remains. In July the slide was still over 30 feet deep and was solid ice. In the effort to find Dollie, considerable blasting was resorted to, a very expensive endeavor. She was finally found on July 26th, almost seven months after her icy death, and after many days of extremely hard work by Charles Anesi, Billy Tonioli, Phil Flynn, Harry Lazarus, Richard McLeod, and others. McLeod's dog was credited with finding the body by his constant digging directly above the spot where Dollie was found. Her body was still entirely covered by snow, but one of her feet was near the surface six or eight inches under the snow. She had been carried 1500 feet in the slide and was in a fair state of preservation, as she had been covered with snow and frozen for seven months.

Dollie Bennett, the former Dollie McCabe of Creede, Colorado, was born in Kansas; she was the sister of Mrs. William Rose of Pueblo, Colorado, and the daughter of James C. Blossom of Bloomfield, Nebraska, formerly of Pueblo, Colorado, who could not be located.

At one time Dollie had been employed by Mrs. George Noll at the Central House Hotel in Silverton, and was held in high esteem by all who knew her. Her husband had worked around the area off and on several years and was well known. Both young people, just in their prime, were very well liked.

Dollie's funeral was held July 31, 1916, at McLeod Undertaking Parlor. Of all the fatal accidents in the history of San Juan County, not one cast more gloom nor aroused greater public sympathy and sorrow than the tragic deaths of the young wife and her husband, whose heroic effort to save her cost him his own life. Dollie's casket was engulfed in a profusion of flowers, the last tribute of affection from her Silverton friends.

A card of thanks was published from her friend, Leta Crabill (or Krehbiel) White, the wife of Bob White, one of the men who was with Dollie and Harvey when they were caught in the slide. She thanked those who contributed to help defray the expense of the funeral, and the search for Dollie's body ... "In life she was my friend, in death I could not forsake her." Bob and Leta had been married August 12, 1915, in Silverton.

**BERGIN, MATTHEW** - Suicide
No Marker - Died Aug 5, 1911 - Age 54 Years - Matthew died from an overdose of morphine at his home. A few years previously he had met with a horrible accident while working in a sawmill, and lost both his hands. He had lived in Silverton only a few months and had been very despondent since his arrival. Born in Pennsylvania, he was unmarried and unemployed. Survivors were two sisters and a brother (not named); his funeral was held at Prosser's Undertaking Parlor in Silverton, and burial took place at Hillside.

**BIELEFELDT, EMIEL** - Scarlet Fever
No Marker - Died Jan 9, 1881 - Emiel, the bright and beautiful little 4-1/2 year old son of the William Bielefeldts, died of scarlet fever on a Sunday in January. Just 19 days after Emiel's death, his 3-1/2 year old sister, Luiese, also died, and the next year, 1882, another Bielefeldt child died; all three children died of scarlet fever, an often fatal disease at the time.

**BLAICH, MARTIN** - Typhoid
No Marker - Died June 14, 1874 - Age about 25 Years - Martin died of typhoid fever out in the mountains. His friend, George Wilson, buried him and later recalled Martin's grave as

being in a lonely and secluded spot between Animas Forks and Burns Gulch. The two friends had come from the midwest to the San Juan and were looking forward to a summer of prospecting in the mountains. Blaich had spent the previous winter in Del Norte, Colorado. His parents lived in Franklin, Missouri, and the one to whom he had pledged his love lived in Illinois. George Wilson noted in 1878 that the burial site, neatly fenced, was then covered with grass, a plain board telling the date of death. No trace remains.

**BLATTNER, SAMUEL "UNCLE SAMMY"**
No Marker - Died July 20, 1899 - Age 75 Years - Uncle Sam died shortly before 9:00 on a Thursday night at Trembath's Boarding House, where he had been very sick for over a week. He suffered from the infirmities of a hard life and old age.

Sam was born in Switzerland and had come to the United States in the mid-1850s. He came to Silverton in the 1870s, one of the early pioneers, and worked as a cook to finance his ventures in prospecting and mining in the hills, near and far. The Uncle Sam claim on Boulder Mountain was one of his more successful locations, and when he sold it for a few hundred dollars, Sam was "in clover" for a couple of years. Later, being destitute, Uncle Sammy became a San Juan County charge and crossed the range (died) as such. He was regarded as a kind-hearted, inoffensive old man. His funeral was held at the undertaking parlor, with burial at Hillside on Boulder Mountain, the mountain upon which he had prospected for many years. It was thought Sam might have two daughters surviving him "across the big waters".

**BOSCHI, JOHN** - Snowslide
No Marker 1877 - Feb 16, 1915 - Age 38 Years - The remains of John, killed in a huge snowslide near the midway terminal of the Arpad tram, were found three months later, in May 1915, by some miners who worked at the Big Giant Mine.

On the morning of February 16th, John received his paycheck at the Black Prince Mine and started to town. A fierce storm was raging and his friends begged him not to go until the storm subsided, but John was determined to make the trip and could not be persuaded otherwise. The men supposed he had reached his destination in safety until the following week when they learned he had not reached Silverton. It was known that the big slide near the midway had run and it was assumed he had been caught and killed in the slide. Friends made futile searches to find his body, but were unsuccessful until the melting snows of spring revealed it.

John, unmarried, was born in Italy and had lived in the Silverton area about twelve years, where his cousin, Henry Boschi, also lived. The funeral and burial took place May 27, 1915.

## BOSS, BESSIE

(20) - Mar 16, 1896 - Aug 31, 1896 - Age 5 Months - Bessie's wooden marker is inscribed "Little Bessie, Daughter of Mr. and Mrs. G. Boss. Rest in Peace Our Darling". A permanent marker for Bessie was donated in 1985, supplementing the wooden marker, still legible at that time. No obituary was found for little Bessie, the only child of George and Rose Boss. Bessie's father, George Boss, achieved fame as mail carrier and stage driver between Red Mountain and Ouray over an extremely treacherous road. He was a short man with a mustache, and was noted for the big hat he usually wore. He was born in 1854 in Illinois, moved to Kansas as a child and to Colorado in 1879. He first lived in what became Montrose County, but was then Gunnison County, and in a year or two settled

in the Silverton area. Over the years he experienced everything possible (except death) in snowslides, and was dubbed "The San Juan Snowslide Rider". He had been covered up and buried, knocked from the trail, with and without his horse and trapped between slides, but he always made the trip and carried the mail, frequently in deadly, blinding blizzards.

In late January 1900, as he was driving the Silverton and Red Mountain stage (which in winter was a sleigh), George met with an accident which very nearly cost him his life. Just below Red Mountain City, the drag chain from the stage caught on a rock, bringing the sleigh to such a sudden stop George was pitched over the front end and landed on the pole between the horses. Fortunately, the animals were gentle and did not kick at what they must have considered a very strange turn of events. Beyond a few bruises, Boss was not injured.

In 1910 *The Silverton Standard* newspaper published a salute to George Boss, noting that in the early days when trails were blocked, the only means of transportation between the isolated and snowbound mining camps was through the heroic stage drivers and mail carriers who would face death in the howling blizzard or the death dealing white terror (snowslides). Not one of them left the camp without many fervent prayers for a safe journey, and not one received a more hearty welcome at his return. During the 1910 blockade the town had seen a vivid example of that early day heroism through the efforts of veteran stage driver and respected old time resident, George Boss. He took it upon himself voluntarily, to break the trail to Red Mountain and bring back the first mail of the blockade. The trip was as hazardous as any ever made. He had encountered the same old dangers, the same old privations, and surmounted the same old difficulties, and finally arrived back safely with his small consignment of mail. In the old days, the whole town would have turned out to meet him with brass and cymbals, but times had changed, and such heroism passed almost unnoticed in 1910.

In February 1914 at the age of 60 years, George was still able to bring the mail through by himself where others had failed. He had cleared up all the Ouray mail accumulated on the other side of the range since the six weeks long blockade and brought to Silverton five heavy sacks on a Sunday afternoon, and as many more the next Wednesday. The newspaper noted that when it came to snow bucking and getting through, even old time railroaders would do well to take a lesson from George! At that time he was said to look about 35 years old, had neither crow's feet nor gray hairs, and always met care with a smile; he was a favorite with all the old timers and a general favorite throughout the San Juan. In June of that same year, 1914, George took a force of men up to Chattanooga for the purpose of clearing and making the road passable for a wagon. In some places the men shoveled snow which was still five feet deep.

It appears that George's first wife, Rose, the mother of little Bessie, died on December 29, 1897, at the age of 26 years, probably in Ouray, where she was buried. In 1918 George moved to a ranch near Bountiful, Utah. Three years later, at the age of 67 years, George married Mrs. Andy Bassett in Salt Lake City, Utah. George's new wife was the grandmother of Miss Amy Colmer, who attended the wedding, along with other former Silverton people.

**BOWEN, WILLIAM C. "BILL"** - Husband of "Sage Hen" or "Aunt Jane" Bowen, the "Pioneer Madam of Blair Street"
(2) - Died June 22, 1891 - Age 61 Years -

Inscribed on his tombstone is "Born in Providence, Rhode Island, At Rest". Bill died of miners consumption. He had been sick for years and the previous winter had gone to California, hoping the change of climate would benefit his health. He was buried at Hillside Cemetery where his grave is identified by a beautiful white marble marker.

Bill had lived in San Juan County many years, having come in the 1870s. He and his wife, Jane, may have lived in Kansas before coming to Colorado; the 1880 census lists their daughter, Eunice, age 13, as having been born in Kansas. A later source noted that Eunice was their adopted daughter.

After the Bowens arrived in Silverton they were granted a liquor license and opened a saloon and dance hall. Dance halls also usually had prostitutes ("pros") available, and Bill's wife, Jane, was known as "The Pioneer Madam of Blair Street". Bill also operated a ranch, consisting of a saloon and boarding house, about 17 miles south of Silverton and three miles north of Cascade, on the Animas Toll Road. There, in 1881, Bill Bowen shot and killed John Haley, who worked for him, because of disagreements over money. The men had been quarreling several days and

Haley, being under the influence of liquor, began to abuse Bowen in a most scurrilous manner, calling him everything he could put his tongue to that was vile and insulting. Bowen accused Haley of stealing from him, and on the day of Haley's death, the two had engaged in several rough fights. Bowen was thoroughly beaten by Haley and after the last beating, Haley told Bowen he would kill him before midnight, then went to his cabin for a weapon.

Haley was a large and powerful man, while Bowen was weak and sickly and suffered from miners con. Haley returned with his hand in his pocket, and Bowen was sitting on a table, holding a revolver. Several men standing by warned Bowen to look out or he'd be killed. Haley lunged for Bowen, who told him to stay back, but Haley kept coming, so Bowen shot him near the heart. Haley continued to advance so Bowen shot him twice more, and Haley finally fell to the floor, dead. Bowen was brought to trial and found innocent, as the jury believed the killing was done in self defense.

Bill's very colorful wife, Jane Bowen, was often called "Sage Hen" and/or "Aunt Jane". She was born in England, but nothing was known of her life there, except that she had lived in the densely populated section on London's East Side, known as Petticoat Lane. In Silverton, she was often summoned into court, but appears to have been quite popular with the Blair Street population of prostitutes, gamblers and saloon keepers, and with the miners and others who patronized her establishment.

At one time her dance hall, the "Westminster", was referred to as "Aunt Jane's Abode for the Fallen", and Ludwig Vota's place nearby was "A Palace of Debauchery". Aunt Jane brought the first variety show to Silverton in 1875, with Bert Clifford as end man.

A newspaper article in February 1895, described a visit to "Aunt Jane's": "We suddenly found ourselves on the premises of Jane Bowen. We paused a moment to listen and observe the persons who frequent such resorts. It was a strange mixture of erring youth, vigorous manhood and grinning decay. Young boys were there, for whom the mother's heart had long been yearning. The hardy sons of toil were there, and old men with turned heads and unsteady steps, all in the mad whirl and excitement of the moment, forgetting the past, present and future. And over all, bedecked in costly jewels, presided the goddess of the evening (Jane Bowen). The proprietress informed us that business was not very good in her line, and that instead of operating a prosperous business, she kept the establishment more as a house of refuge and rest for the fallen ones of earth, driven to desperation and despair through man's depravity. Such was life in the far west."

After her husband's death in 1891, Jane sold her property in Silverton to Joe Sartore and left for England; she soon returned to Silverton, and in 1895 discovered someone had put carbolic acid into her food (it didn't kill her). A nephew who had recently departed for Brooklyn, was suspected of the deed.

In 1898 Jane received a telegram announcing the death of her daughter in Denver. Eunice, also referred to as Emma and Emily, was 28 years old at the time of her death, and had been well educated; however she was in ill health and became despondent because she couldn't work. She ended her life by ingesting the poison "Rough on Rats" while she was living at St. Catherine's Home.

In December 1899, Jane, who had been visiting relatives in London, returned to

Silverton, and again in 1902 Jane returned to Silverton after a two year visit to London. She started up her "Palace Dance Hall" on the corner of 12th and Blair Streets, and once again her familiar voice would admonish the uproarious throng not to "lift the roof off me 'ouse!" She announced that she would conduct her dance hall business in the good old-fashioned way .. good music, fine floor and "Aunt Jane says, boys from the 'ills hare hinvited to call 'round hand take ha glass hat 'er hexpense!" Nothing was found to indicate when Aunt Jane permanently left Silverton, where she went or when she died.

**BRACCO, JOE** - Suicide - Cut his Own Throat
No Marker - May 8, 1888 - Apr 20, 1920 - Age 32 Years - The previous winter Joe got mixed up in a fight and never fully recovered from the severe blow inflicted to his head at that time. He was acting queerly and had not been seen at his usual haunts for several days, and his friends, becoming alarmed, decided to search for him. They found his frozen body on the Red Mountain railroad track between Silverton and Burro Bridge, opposite the Thompson bungalow. Poor Joe had used a knife to cut his own throat (through the windpipe), sometime between April 19th and

23rd. Coroner O'Halloran brought the poor soul's body to town.

Born in San Benigno, Italy, Joe had no known relatives in America. His funeral, held at McLeod Undertaking Parlor under the auspices of the Foresters of America, was attended by a large number of friends, and burial at Hillside followed the service.

**BRAMMEIER, GEORGE W.** - Suicide (23) - Nov 24, 1879 - Jan 16, 1961 - Age 81 Years - George died at 11:50 a.m., about 1-1/2 hours after shooting himself in the head at the rear of 1364 Reese Street. The bullet entered his right temple and emerged at his left temple. He had been in reasonably good health but didn't want to become a burden to anyone in his old age.

George had lived in Silverton nearly 30 years and was born in Henderson, Iowa, the son of Jacob Brammeier. When he was a few years old the family moved to the San Luis Valley in Colorado, and his father worked at the now forgotten mining camp of Wassen, near Creede. As mining dwindled following the Silver Panic of 1892, the family moved to Naturita, Colorado, where they became permanent residents.

George was an industrious hard-working and thrifty person all his life. In the Naturita area he worked at ranching and drove four-horse teams belonging to his brother, Cleve (Thomas Cleveland) Brammeier, hauling uranium to the railroad siding at Placerville. The roads were all dirt and the heavy ore wagons would often bog down in the mud. Each round trip took about six days. Before coming to Silverton in 1929, he worked in Telluride hauling lumber to the Smuggler Mine and spent a season in Yellowstone driving a team for the road construction in West Yellowstone. His first work in the Silverton area was at the Sunnyside Mill, where he worked as an operator, and after the mill closed down he worked at various mines in the district. His last regular employment was at the Shenandoah Mill where he worked many years before his retirement in about 1951.

A good citizen, quiet and unassuming, George liked Silverton and had many friends with whom he associated daily. He was an accomplished mechanic, well known for repairing old clocks, often making his own parts. He was an avid sportsman and the best posted person in town on baseball and other sports. In the summer he often made fishing trips to the high lakes, trips that would have been a challenge to men half his age, and up until a few months before his death, he drove his own car, a 1930 Ford, which he purchased new when he lived in Eureka.

Survivors were his brothers, John, in Nevada, "Cleve" and Henry of Ridgway, Colorado, and sisters, Mrs. P.L. Ray of Denver and Mrs. Howard Grimes of Nucla, Colorado. The funeral was held at Maguire Funeral Chapel, Rev. Marvin Hudson officiating. Helene Bausman Crawford and her daughter, Norma Crawford Wyman, rendered the funeral music. Honorary pallbearers were Pete Motto, Jess Carey, Blaz Rodman and Charles Hawkins; active pallbearers were Jim Baudino, Aldo Bonavida, Bud Bertram, "Deacon" Salfisberg, Joe Arietta and Ross Beaber, all close friends of George. Burial was at Hillside; five years later, in 1966, George's brother, Henry, also shot himself; their brother, Cleve, died in 1969, and the three Brammeier brothers are buried side by side at Hillside.

George's friend, Ross Beaber, publisher of the newspaper in Silverton, noted that "For 20 years George seemed a part of our family. For 20 years he never missed being at our home for Thanksgiving and Christmas and other special occasions. When we were out of town we knew the office stokes would be properly attended. We tried to return the favors but were always lagging behind. We took his advice on repairing machinery at the print shop. He was a genius at making intricate parts such as are often needed on linotypes and feeders. George never missed a day coming to the shop, sitting in his favorite chair and reading his favorite exchanges, topmost of which was the *Montrose Press*, which reported happenings of his old home town of Naturita. If good honorable living is rewarded with eternal life and happiness, George should receive a top award. He had all the qualifications."

**BRAMWELL, WILLIAM** - Mine Accident No Marker - Died Dec 8, 1882 - Age 28 Years - William, a native of Cardiganshire, Wales, died from injuries suffered in a 90 foot fall down an open shaft at the Aspen Mine on Hazelton Mountain. His candle went out at about 5:00 on a Thursday afternoon and he stepped into the open shaft in the dark mine. Both his legs and an arm were broken in the fall, in addition to sustaining very serious injuries to his spine. He suffered horribly until death came to the relief of his tortured mangled body about ten hours later.

The entire force from the mine came down for his funeral at the Congregational Church, and marched in the procession to the grave. There were no known survivors.

**BREEN, MARIA JULIANITA "JULIA" TOBIN** (20) - Oct 12, 1850 - Dec 13, 1926 - Age 76 Years - After a lingering illness, Julia died in Silverton at the home of her daughter, Maggie (Mrs. Charles Melton). Her funeral was held from her former residence, with Rev. A.C. Best officiating, and she was buried beside her husband, Mickey Breen, at Hillside. Her marker was donated in 1995.

Maria Julianita was the daughter of Tom and Pasquala Bermal Tobin. The obituary information, furnished by her youngest daughter, Margaret Breen Melton, at whose home she died, stated she was born at Fort Garland, Colorado, but other sources indicated she was born near Taos, New Mexico. (Fort Garland was not built until 1858, eight years after Julia's birth. Fort Garland replaced nearby Fort Massachusetts, which was established in 1852; the two forts were built to keep the Indians from impeding settlement of the San Luis Valley. Construction was begun in 1851 with founding of the town of San Luis by Hispanics from New Mexico. Kit Carson commanded Fort Garland in 1866 and 1867, as an officer in the New Mexico Volunteers. The fort was abandoned in 1883.)

Julia's father, Missouri-born Tom Tobin, was a remarkable personality and one of the most famous pioneer scouts and Indian fighters. A close friend of Kit Carson, he scouted for the G.A.R. (Grand Army of the Republic) several years and was advance scout for General Fremont on his historical trip to the west coast. He was also a trail blazer for wagon trains making their way west, throughout all the early history of Colorado and the west.

Tom Tobin was noted for his daring exploits and the remarkable skill with which he tracked and finally slew two Mexican fanatics whose fiendish plan was to kill every white person who came their way. Their expedition led from New Mexico through Fremont, El Paso and Park Counties, Colorado, and their pathway was strewn with corpses. A veritable reign of terror followed their foul deeds. Only one person who saw them was left alive to tell the tale, and when that man told his story in Fairplay, Colorado, a search party was formed. After a long search the two bandits were found in a mountain camp; one was killed, but the other escaped.

In the fall of that same year, 1863, the bandit who escaped re-entered the area bent on the same murderous mission, and when he eluded capture by the troops, the old scout, Tom Tobin, was put on the trail. In five days time, Tom tracked the bandit and his partner to their camp in the mountains, killed both of them and cut off their heads. He put the heads in a sack, threw it across his saddle and took the heads to Fort Garland where they were exhibited to the garrison. Tom Tobin died in 1904 at Fort Garland, Colorado, at the age of 90 years.

On January 14, 1866, at La Costilla, New Mexico, in the Chapel of Saint Michael, Julia Tobin, age 15, married Michael Breen, a 30 year old Civil War veteran. The six children born to Mickey and Julia were John, Mary, Amelia Frances "Emma", Maggie, Julia, and another son, Thomas, who died in 1881 when he was eleven years old; he is buried at Hillside. In 1877 Mickey Breen moved his mercantile business to Silverton. Julia and the children continued to live mainly at Fort Garland, and Michael lived mostly in Silverton, although all members of the family visited back and forth. The children were bilingual, as their mother spoke only Spanish.

Julia's husband, Michael Breen, died in 1894; she had never lived in Silverton before that time, but after Michael's death, Julia contracted with F.O. Sherwood to tear down Michael's old house and build her a new five room house on the lot. She furnished her new home with elegant furniture from Prosser's Furniture Store, and she spent the rest of her life in Silverton.

**BRENNAN, THOMAS** - Snowslide
No Marker - 1852 - Feb 2, 1883 - Age 30 Years - The deadly slide made its power felt when a man and ten mules perished in its icy embrace    The snow had been falling continuously several days and was heavy on the mountainsides.    February 2nd was an unusually warm day and at about noon, the Stafford muletrain was packing ore from the Yankee Girl Mine to Sweetville.  On the trail to the mine, the procession was engulfed in a snowslide which crashed down from the rocky cliffs 300 feet above the trail.  Tom Brennan, Jim Barr and 13 mules were swallowed and buried by the snow, ice and debris.

The men from the Yankee Girl Mine were soon on the ground with shovels, working their hardest to rescue the unfortunate men and animals.  About half an hour after the slide had run, alongside a dead mule, Jim Barr was found buried under six feet of snow, still alive, and was brought to consciousness in about ten minutes. The 50 men continued digging feverishly, looking for Brennan, but he was not found until the next day.

Tom was from Lake Village, Indiana, where his mother still lived. It was not often the community was called upon to attend a triple funeral, but such was the case on the Monday when Rev. S.H. Cheadle preached a funeral service over the remains of Thomas M. Brennan, Robert B. Barton and Frank Wyatt.

Barton, age about 25, died at Red Mountain Town of inflammation of the bowels, and after the funeral, his body was shipped to his parents at Neodesha, Kansas.

Frank Wyatt, age about 55 years, died of pneumonia at the Columbia (or Alaska) Mine. He was from Georgia where it was believed he had a family. Wyatt and Tom Brennan were both buried at Hillside on a cold February day. The procession was a scene to be long remembered; each body was pulled through the deep snow on a sled, then lowered into the graves on the mountainside.

**BROCKENAUER, FRED, JR.** - Pneumonia (9) - Apr 17, 1896 - May 6, 1915 - Age 19 Years - Once again the angel of death entered the Fred Brockenauer home and bore away on relentless wings the manly soul of their oldest son. Two weeks previously he had come home from his work at the Sunnyside Mill suffering from a severe cold. After about a week he felt quite improved and returned to work, only to suffer a relapse which soon developed into pneumonia and proved fatal.

Fred, born in Silverton, was the oldest of the seven Brockenauer children, four of whom had died previously (two in Silverton, two in Durango). The remains of Walter and another brother, William C., both buried in Durango, were disinterred and brought to Silverton the night after their brother, Fred, died; the three brothers were then buried in the family plot at Hillside beside their two infant sisters who died in 1897 and 1899. Fred was a member of the Woodmen of the World and his insurance policy with that order left $1,000 to his mother.

Survivors were his parents, Fred and Therese Brockenauer (both born in Germany); his sister, Marguerite, and his brother, Karl, all of Silverton.

The funeral was held at Miners Union Hall under the auspices of the Woodmen of the World; the service was most impressive and the large attendance and beautiful floral offerings gave evidence of the high esteem in which young Fred was held by the community. The Woodmen of the World escorted the remains to the cemetery, and upon returning, escorted the bereaved parents to their home. Mrs. Brockenauer, broken by the harsh blows dealt to her in life, died less than a year later.

The Brockenauer family plot is near the road, with a large gray stone for Therese Doepel Brockenauer, the mother, facing the road. Markers for the Brockenauer children were donated in 1986.

**BROCKENAUER, THERESE DOEPEL**
(9) - Oct 17, 1869 - Apr 14, 1916 - Age 46 Years - Therese, a devoted and kind wife and mother, had been dealt much sorrow and suffering by her own ill health and the tragic deaths of five of her seven children. Acute mania was noted as the cause of her death.

Born in Germany, she had come to Silverton in 1893, where she and Fred Brockenauer, a well known carpenter in the area, were married on July 6, 1895, and "like sensible folks, the young couple went to housekeeping at once". Little did they know the tragedies life had in store for them. Children born to them were: Fred, Jr. in 1896 who died in 1915; a daughter born and died in 1897; another little girl in 1898, who died in 1899; Walter born May 1900 and died in 1913; William C., born in 1912 and died in 1913; the two children who did not die were Marguerite, born November 20, 1902, and Karl, born February 3, 1906.

Survivors of Therese were her husband, Fred, and her daughter and son, Marguerite, age 14 years, and Karl, age 10 years. Her funeral was held at Miners Union Hall under the auspices of the Women of Woodcraft with Rev. R.C. Byers officiating. Therese, who had lived through so much tragedy, was buried at Hillside beside five of her children who preceded her in death. Her marker, a large gray granite stone, faces the lower road. The Womans Benefit Association of the Maccabees, of which she was a member, also installed their marker which bears the likeness of a woman, child and dog.

*"She resteth now.*
*No more her breast heaves*
*with its weary breath;*
*Pain sits no longer on the brow*

*where lies the calm of death.*
*Sunk to her rest like a tired child,*
*She lies in slumber deep,*
*Soft folded in the arms of Him*
*Who giveth tranquil sleep.* "

**BROWN, JAMES** - Inflammation of Bowels
(4) - No Marker - Died Dec 11, 1889 - James,
an old timer in Silverton, died of inflammation
of the bowels on an early Wednesday morning.
He had been working at the North Star Mine
on King Solomon Mountain for some months
past, and for about two weeks had been far
from well, but would not lay down the
hammer. Saturday noon he was compelled to
take to his bed, and three friends went down
from the mine to Silverton early Sunday
morning, searching for a doctor; it was
storming too hard for anyone to go up. On
Monday Jim's friend, Kilburn, returned alone
to the mine through the deep snow, and the
next day, Tuesday, several men brought the
sick man down to town. They reached
Silverton at 6:00 that evening, and after taking
some stimulants, Brown revived a little. At
10:00 o'clock that night he appeared to be a
little better, but in reply to Charley Snowden's
question as to how he felt, James replied,
"Charley, I'm going fast". His words proved

only too true.  At midnight he was much weaker and at 2:20 he fell asleep in Jesus, conscious to the last.  His brothers, Frank and Mike Brown, were with him when death came.

Jim,  born in Ireland, came to Silverton in about 1886, where his brothers, Mike and Frank, also settled. He was well known to everyone in the Silverton section, and every man with whom he associated spoke of him with words of praise.  He was regarded as industrious, honest and all that a man could be.

Survivors included brothers and sisters in Kansas, New Jersey, New Zealand, the old country, and in Silverton.  The funeral was held on a Thursday afternoon, with a large number of friends following the remains up the hill to his last resting place at Hillside.

## BROWN, WILLIAM P.

(4) - Died Mar 1, 1899 - When this little boy died  at the age of two months, the bereaved parents, Frank and Kate Brown, had the sympathy of the entire community.  Survivors were his parents, his brother, Frank, Jr., and his sister, Nellie Jane (who later married Howard Hill).  The parents published a card of thanks in the newspaper after the death of their baby, and especially thanked "Happy Jack"

Shaeffer, who risked his life in a perilous trip over the snowslides acting as a messenger in the cause of humanity.

"Happy Jack" left the Tom Jones Saloon at Middleton on Wednesday morning, March 1st, at 4:00 o'clock, headed for the Ridgway Mine, three miles distant, to tell Frank Brown his baby boy was dangerously ill. Jack, on snowshoes (skis) took what was known as the Golden Lake Route, which was supposed to be less dangerous than the old route up the gulch. He climbed the high range to the right of the gulch, and six hours later, at about 10:00 o'clock was well skyward, way above timberline, within 500 yards of the Ridgway workings, just over a high wedge shaped peak. The incline was so steep that Jack took off his snowshoes and climbed a few steps.

Suddenly, the snow broke from under his feet and with the speed of lightning went crashing downward about 200 feet, carrying the case-hardened old prospector along with it. Fortunately, when the slide came to a stop, Jack's head was above the snow and he could breathe. Miraculously, he suffered no injury except for being "skeered". Bowing himself out of the dangerous embrace of the snow "with no snowshoes, no nuthin" he waded through chin deep snow the rest of that day. Just as darkness engulfed him, he made it to Gottlieb's cabin, where he stayed until morning, ultimately reaching the Ridgway Mine at 9:00 a.m. on Thursday, March 2nd. He had been 29 hours traveling three miles, and several of his fingers were badly frozen.

"Happy Jack" and Frank Brown, the sick baby's father, arrived back in town that evening and found, tragically, the baby had died on the day "Happy Jack" started on his dangerous mission of mercy. A few years later, in 1906, "Happy Jack" was blown to atoms in a blasting accident, and his remains brought to Silverton in a couple of canvas sacks.

**BRUENDER, ANDREW** - Also Known as Andrew Anderson - Mine Explosion
No Marker - Died Dec 10, 1903, 4:00 p.m. - Age about 32 Years - While working at the Sunnyside Mine, Andrew, a Finlander, drilled into a missed shot and was instantly killed by the explosion. His working partner had just gone to another part of the tunnel and by so doing escaped his companion's awful fate. Bruender's body was terribly mangled, the head being almost torn from the trunk.

He had formerly lived at Telluride, was single, about 35 years old, and had been at the Sunnyside about three weeks. He had no known relatives in America, and was to have been buried by the Miners Union; however, when it was found he was not a member in good standing financially (had not paid his dues), the Union would not participate. Mr. Terry, superintendent of the Sunnyside Mine, then volunteered to pay the cost of burial and Andrew was buried at Hillside.

### BRUNN, CARL - Snowslide
No Marker - Died Jan 2, 1910 - Age 40 Years
A severe storm had been raging two days, with a heavy fall of very wet snow. The next day it grew colder with high winds and soon developed into a howling blizzard which lasted another four days as the temperature fell to 34 degrees below zero. The peculiar conditions of the storm convinced those familiar with weather conditions in the area, that it not only meant a serious blockade, but also the running of many snowslides. Already, on the day of New Year's Eve, Art Rice had been caught and killed in a gigantic slide on Houghton Mountain. Carl was to meet a similar fate.

Carl had just gone off shift at the Iowa Mill in Arrastra Basin, and was in his cabin building a fire when, without warning, a mountain of snow hit the cabin, crushing it and everything in it, including Carl, like eggshells. His remains were later recovered from under eight feet of snow and ice.

No one knew anything of Carl's relatives, as he was a recent arrival in the county from Norway, although one source noted he had lived in Silverton two years. He was buried at Hillside January 5, 1910, far from home and loved ones.

## BUCKLEY, WILLIAM EDGAR
No Marker - Died Mar 11, 1906 - Age 38 Years - William, who worked as a musician at one of the town dance halls, died in the rooming house above Sherman's Saloon. He went to bed late, a little the worse for liquor, but not otherwise ailing. The next morning, the chambermaid got no response when she went to awaken him, and when the door was forced open, he was found dead in bed.

A native of Nebraska, Walter was a man of more than ordinary education and refinement. Survivors were his mother and a sister in Butte, Montana, and a brother in Pueblo, Colorado. His funeral was held from Prosser Undertaking and burial was at Hillside.

**BURGHUS, FRANCIS** - Murdered - First Known Death in San Juan County - Also Spelled Bergess, Burgess, Borghus

No Marker - Died sometime before June 17, 1872 - His death was noted in 1883 when men coming through the Cement Creek country observed the following notice posted near the wagon road opposite Ross Basin:

"'Buried here a man by the name of Francis Burghus. Was killed by parties unknown and found on the 17th day of June, 1872, and buried on this very spot.' Who he was and when he was murdered was not known; perhaps someone would be gratified to know of the passing of this lonely one."

**BURNELL, LAURA** - Car Wreck

(20) - May 2, 1908 - Aug 27, 1923 - Age 15 Years - Laura, oldest daughter of the Robert Burnells, was instantly killed when the car in which she was riding with seven young friends, plunged several hundred feet down the cliffs and into the river about four miles from Silverton, near Howardsville. Others in the car were the driver, Tom Slade, Jr., Ward Dodson, Bill Mullin, Domenica and Mary Chiono, Ida Bosworth and Laura Lorenzon. Shortly before the accident, the happy group left Silverton to drive to Eureka. They met a

car coming from the other direction at a point where the road curved sharply, and their car veered off the narrow road. The others were thrown free of the car and escaped with minor injuries, but Laura was crushed to death when the car hit the sharp boulders.

Occupants of the other car, Evelyn Gooch and Messrs. Colson and Stamphel (Stampfel), immediately stopped to help the victims, and Stamphel rushed on to Silverton for help. While he was gone, the others recovered Laura's body and placed her by the side of the road. A truck from Western Colorado Power was the first to reach the scene from Silverton and transported the body of the unfortunate young girl into town. Laura's death marked the second auto fatality in the county. The first occurred a year earlier when another young woman, Henrietta Barotto, met death in a one-car wreck near Irene Gulch on the Gladstone Road.

Laura was born in Durango at the home of her grandmother, Gwen Roberts Jones Jenkins, and spent her life in Silverton, where she had completed her first year of high school. A highly ambitious girl, she participated in all school activities, and was looking forward to another school year, shortly to begin.

Survivors were her parents, Robert D. and Laura Jones Stanger Burnell; sisters: Alice, Gladys and Gwendolyn Lee Burnell; brother, Robert "Dobbie" Burnell, Jr.; half-brother, William Stanger and half-sister, Blanche Stanger (Mrs. Charles) McMillen.

Business was suspended when the residents of the stricken community assembled at the Congregational Church to pay a last tribute to Laura's memory. The funeral was the largest in recent years and was conducted by Rev. John Everington of Durango. Escorted by her classmates and friends, her body was taken to Hillside Cemetery as the shadows of approaching evening were falling on the mountains, and she was committed to the earth for her long and endless rest.

**CONKLIN, INFANT BOY** - Died 1897 - Son of Walter B. and Mrs. Conklin
No Marker - Jan 12, 1896 - Jan 24, 1897 - Age 1 Year - This child's little shoes and clothes would be carefully packed away and treasured as mementos of the darling boy that once lived. The baby was sick with croup about two days before his life was snuffed out. His funeral was held at the home of his bereaved parents on Greene Street, with burial at Hillside. The little one had brought great

happiness and shown unusual promise ... but now he was gone.

## DALLAVALLE, GUISEPPE (DALLA, JOE)
- Mine Explosion
(1) - 1857 - Nov 21, 1897 - Age 40 Years - Joe, an Austrian, was killed at the Iowa Mine at about 7:30 on a Sunday morning while drilling a missed hole fired by the previous shift. No one told him that the charge had missed firing and it was just after coming on shift when he went in and started drilling. The old drilling was 6 to 8 inches deep, and from the explosion that followed about his third stroke of the hammer, it appeared to have contained at least a quarter of a charge of giant powder. When found, Joe was headless, nothing but the chin and lower part of his right ear remaining. He could not have known what hit him as his head was literally blown to pieces. The newspaper noted it was the same old story .. carelessness on the part of the miner. His body was loaded onto the tram and taken to Coroner Prosser's undertaking rooms where it was prepared for burial. No inquest was held.

Survivors included his brother in Silverton, John Dalla, and his wife and four children in Tyrol. He had lived in the area about two years and had won the confidence and good will of all with whom he associated, mainly the hardy and patient toilers underground. He was a bright, energetic, likeable fellow for so horrible a fate.

Joe (Guiseppe) Dallavalle was the maternal grandfather of Silverton resident Joe Todeschi, and his tombstone inscription is on a white marble marker shared with Angelo (Tony) Todeschi, who was later moved to Sector (5) of the cemetery; also inscribed on the marker is Joe Todeschi 1865-1897.

The day after his death 75 men of the Iowa working force, as well as his relatives and friends, attended Joe's funeral at the Catholic Church, followed by burial at Hillside.

In the same newspaper which reported Joe's tragic and awful death, was an article describing another mine accident two days later: Walter Eales and John Olson received horrible injuries while picking a missed hole at the Silver Lake Mine. Their faces and necks were horribly gashed and lacerated and their eyes severely injured. Eales was sure to lose his left eye and the soundness of his right eye was yet in question. His right hand was also very badly mangled. Olson suffered burning from powder about his face and eyes; his hands and left knee were very badly cut up. "It seems that after the many examples that have been set, some at so great sacrifice and so disastrous consequences, more precaution ought to be taken by the miners in the case of missed holes ... but it is evident that they do not profit by the experience of their fellows."

*"Only a miner, killed in a breath,*
*only a working man, gone to his death,*
*only a grave 'neath a murmuring pine,*
*Joe, aged 40, killed in a mine."*

## DERMODY, JAMES - Shot

(17) - Died May 27, 1879 - Age 35 Years - Another victim of the evil effects of whiskey, James, a warm-hearted Irishman, lost his life at Goode's Saloon. He and his brother, Peter, had been on a spree the night before at Bowen's Saloon, and were persuaded by Hi Ward, the one-armed night watchman, to go home. The next night they were celebrating and drinking again at Goode's Saloon and good naturedly got into a scuffle between themselves. Hi Ward again repeatedly tried to get them to go home, and failing this, he threatened to arrest them and lock them up. Ward reached for James, but James, boisterous and feeling no pain, caught Ward's finger in his teeth, wrapped an arm around his neck and

called for the rest of the boys in the saloon to help him lock up the night watchman. In the ensuing scuffle, Ward ended up on his back in the ditch with several of the crowd sitting on him. Angrily, and probably a little scared, Hi Ward drew his pistol and fired, striking and killing the irrepressible, fun-loving Irishman, James Dermody.

Survivors in America were his two brothers, Peter, who was with him at the time of the unfortunate event, and Michael, who lived at Mt. Sneffels where he had interest in the Yankee Boy and other mines. The funeral took place May 31, 1879, and was largely attended.

When sober, Jim was a cheerful, frank, quiet and peaceable man and it was generally felt the shooting by Hi Ward was an unwarranted sacrifice of life. Just three months later, Hi Ward was again involved in another fatal shooting ... that of James M. "Ten Die" Brown. Although Henry Cleary was lynched for that shooting, many felt the bullet which killed Brown may well have come from the gun of Hiram Ward, who had no use for "Ten Die". Hi Ward later left Silverton and returned to Ohio. There, after killing his brother-in-law, he committed suicide in 1883.

The marker for the Dermody brothers is lettered "In Memory of James Dermody, Died at Silverton, Colorado, May 27, 1876 (this should correctly read 1879), Age 35 Years; Peter Dermody, Died at Cantonment on Uncompahgre, Colorado, July 26, 1887, Age 42 Years. Natives of Roscrea, County Tipperary, Ireland. May They Rest in Peace. Erected by Their Brother, Michael". Michael, the last of the brothers to die is also buried in the plot, but there were no brothers left to see that his name was inscribed on the marker.

**DUFFIELD, RALPH "BLIND BOSTON"**
No Marker - 1886 - Mar 8, 1939 - Age 53 Years - Until a few days before his death at Denver General Hospital, Ralph had worked at his news stand in front of the Elks building at 14th and California Streets in Denver. He was born in Boston, Massachusetts, and had come to Colorado in 1903. He made Silverton his home several years, and one former resident remembered him as a stuttering poker player and bartender in Koehler's Saloon. He was generally regarded as a genial, jolly, whole souled person.

In 1915, Ralph started tending bar at the Trimble Springs Hotel, near Durango, and in late summer of that year when he was 29 years old, attempted suicide by shooting himself through the head. No motive was known, but he had been drinking excessively for some time. The bullet didn't kill him, but did blind him. It entered his right temple and passed clear through his head, cutting some of the eye nerves. In 1916, Ralph entered the State Home for the Blind at Denver and his father, supposedly a prominent clergyman of Boston, was to pay all expenses.

For several years Ralph tried anything and everything to have his eyesight restored; his friends in Silverton contributed money toward treatments for him, but Ralph remained sightless. In 1917 the Silverton newspaper advertised hammocks made by "Blind Boston" for sale at reasonable prices at Silverton's Star Theater. In 1920, "Blind Boston" was living in Denver and selling newspapers on the Elks Home corner.

In 1923, when aviation was still quite new, the Denver Post published Ralph's picture and a story of his plane ride over Denver . ."for 12 minutes the people of Denver had to look up to the newsboy". "Blind Boston's" news stand became a landmark and information bureau for San Juan people visiting in Denver and as soon as they hit Denver, they looked him up. In

1925, "Blind Boston" wrote to the Silverton editor, stating that ten years previously, on August 31, 1915, he became "delighted", (meaning blind) and "I can truthfully say that I have been delighted in every sense of the word for the past ten years. I enjoy myself more now than when I had eyes. Then, I used to be like a Greeley potato ... having eyes, I saw not. Now I go to ball games and theaters, taking someone with me to tell what's to be seen. I can hear what is to be heard, and putting the two together, I get the whole story."

In the fall of 1931, "Blind Boston" visited Silverton. He had been blind since 1915, but recognized several Silverton people by their voices, some of whom he had not met since early in his affliction. Others who had seen him in Denver, were recognized as soon as they spoke. A.M. Carlson, a Denver friend, accompanied Ralph on the trip.

Ralph's dying request was that his ashes be scattered around Silverton, for his heart and soul were with Silverton and its people. Mrs. A.M. Close of Denver, a friend of "Blind Boston", shipped the ashes to the newspaper, and members of the Elks Lodge, including Norman Bawden and Art Lorenzon, attended to fulfilling "Blind Boston's" request, by scattering his ashes over his old stomping grounds along Greene and Blair Streets. Survivors were a brother, Wilmington Duffield in Massachusetts, and his step-mother, Mrs. Mary Duffield of Thomasville, Georgia.

**EASLEY, WILLIAM "BILL"** - Suicide by Giant Powder
No Marker - Died June 15, 1905 - Age 50 Years - At about 5:00 on a Thursday afternoon in June, Bill, one of Silverton's well known citizens, ended his career and his life by blasting himself with giant powder. During the past winter he had been imbibing liquor in rather large quantities and was also heavily in debt. Evidently, Bill felt his habit was incurable, and in a temporary fit of insanity, concluded to end his misery and pay his earthly accounts. The deed occurred just outside the city limits near the house he had occupied several years. Frank Deckert, who was coming down the Cement Creek road, had seen Easley come out of his cabin, clad only in underwear, and moments later, he heard the blast and saw a mass of human flesh on the ground. Bill had placed a stick of powder (dynamite) in his waistband, or laid on it, lit it and blew off the left side of his body.

He had come to the San Juan in 1882 and was a man whose generosity was faultless. Although he was known to be addicted to the liquor habit at periods, he was so polite, generous and honest at all times that his good qualities covered the sin that hurt himself most. His remains, in a bad state of mutilation, were "carted off to the potters field at Hillside at the expense of the county". It was as sad as it was shameful. His only survivor was a brother in the Indian Territory.

## ECCHER, GIGI LOUISA - Flu

(6) - April 8, 1894 - Nov 3, 1918 - Age 24 Years - Her marker is lettered "Geegee Eaker 1894 - 1918". No obituary was published for Gigi, a lovely young wife and mother who died in the devastating worldwide flu epidemic which struck as World War I was coming to an end. So many Silverton residents were sick, dying or dead, it was not possible for the newspapers to publish an obituary for each fatality, and instead resorted to publishing lists of the deaths each week. Much of the information for Gigi was furnished in 1992 by her son, Gene Eccher (Ecker) and his wife, Bernice, of Hemet, California.

Gigi's parents, Joseph and Amalia Romano Louisa, were both born in Italy, where they married and lived until about 1890. They immigrated to America and settled in Iron Mountain, Michigan, where Gigi, the eldest of their five children, was born. The family moved to Silverton, Colorado, in 1899, and the father, Joseph, worked in the mines.

Little was found regarding Gigi's life, but she was remembered by long-time Silverton resident, Louie Dalla, as a very beautiful girl. On December 24, 1911, when she was 17, Gigi and James Eccher were married in Silverton by Squire W.D. Watson, Justice of the Peace. Witnesses were Gigi's 12 year old sister, Gracie Louisa, and Matt Dalla. Jim Eccher, the groom, was born August 28, 1890 in Tirol, Austria. The couple's first child, James, Jr., was born prematurely December 31, 1912, and died January 2, 1913; Eugene was born November 14, 1913; Irene Amelia was born March 24, 1915 and died when she was about three weeks old, on April 18, 1915, and Gigi's last child, Ernest John "Bud" was born March 23, 1916.

When stricken with flu, Gigi was visiting in Telluride, but returned to Silverton where she died a few days later. Many flu victims were buried in mass graves, as individual graves could not be dug fast enough. Gigi's burial record states she was buried in a casket in the Louisa family plot by a friend. Before her burial, Gigi's husband, Jim, bundled up his little son, Gene, who was soon to be five years old, and took him to look at his mother for the last time. The memory stayed with Gene, for when he returned to Silverton more than thirty years later, he recognized the building (Miners Union Hall) where he had been taken to see his mother in her casket.

After Gigi's death her husband, took his two sons to live with his sister, Camila Casagranda, in Denver. Gene was five years old and Ernest was a little over two years. Camila, who had a family of her own, placed the boys in St. Vincent's Home for Boys, West 42nd Avenue and Lowell Boulevard, Denver, Colorado. St. Vincent's, operated by the Sisters of Charity, had 280 boys living there in May 1924. Gene and Ernest lived there about six years before they were adopted by Jim and Rosario Pagliuso of Trinidad, Colorado. The boys' adopted names were Eugene and Frank Pagliuso. Musically inclined, they played in Father Zaccardi's Band for five years in Trinidad. The band, associated with Mt. Carmel Church, was called the Mt. Carmel Boys Band. Gene played the trumpet and Frank (Ernest) the clarinet. Years later, the boys learned that while they were growing up in Trinidad, their biological father lived in nearby Victor, Colorado.

After high school, Gene, who then went by his birth name, Eugene Eccher (Ecker), stopped to help a man who was having car trouble on the highway near Trinidad, Colorado. That man turned out to be Joe Case, head of Paramount Movie Studio's scenic department. He very much appreciated Gene's assistance and told him to look him up if he ever needed a job in California. In 1933 Gene set out for California, was hired at Paramount and worked there 45 years, from 1933 until 1978, when he retired. Along the way he became a well known artist, noted for his clown and abstract paintings, which were collected by several Hollywood stars, including Jerry Lewis and Martha Hyer. Gene was known as a man who could get things done in a hurry, when needed. Using a brush or spray gun for two weeks, he'd get 800 gallons of paint onto 65 by 200 foot canvases to be used as scenic backings, mixing his colors in 52 gallon drums. When director Hal Wallis wanted footprints on a ceiling, Gene, or Gaucho, as he was known, had two husky colleagues hold him upside down while he walked on the ceiling, having dipped his feet (in shoes) in paint beforehand.

At one time, Gene was flown to New York to paint zebra stripes on 34 jeeps, a job he completed by hand in five days. Gene received his nickname "Gaucho" from Cecil B. DeMille, while filming in Mexico ... Gene could speak Spanish and translate for the English speaking crew.

In 1938 James Eccher, the boys' natural father, wrote to Colorado authorities asking if it would be possible for him to see his two sons, Eugene and Ernest, as he was not expected to live much longer. The couple who had adopted and raised the two boys, Jim and Rosario Pagliuso, gave their permission and Gene, who had been married two years, and Ernest "Bud", who was 22, were reunited with their natural father. Gene's wife, Bernice, and their two daughters, joined in later visits to the natural father, and they also frequently visited the adoptive parents, Jim and Rosario Pagliuso, who had no other children. Jim Eccher, the natural father, had remarried and was the father of two other sons, Gene (William Eugene) and Robert. The father was remorseful that he had given up his first sons, Gene and Ernest, when they were so very young, and was truly happy to be reunited with them so many years later. He told them "now I can die in peace". The father died in 1942.

Gene's brother, Ernest John "Bud" Eccher, who kept his adopted name of Frank Pagliuso, joined the Air Force in 1938. He served until 1945 and attained the rank of captain. "Bud" was a band leader while in the Air Force and also later in Trinidad, Colorado; he also played and taught violin. Eventually he moved to California where he and his brother, Gene, operated a school photography business. In 1950, while on a Nevada business trip, riding in a car with his assistant, he died of a blood clot to his heart. His death was a severe shock to his brother, Gene (and his family), as the brothers had been extremely close all their lives, having shared a lifetime of heartaches and joys.

For many years, Gene and his brother planned to visit Silverton to learn more of their relatives and place of birth. Sadly, Ernest "Bud" died before that could be accomplished. In 1951, Gene was on a movie location for Paramount in Silverton, and met his uncle and aunt who lived in Silverton, Bryan Louisa and Grace Louisa Motto. Through them Gene learned of many other relatives previously unknown to him and he also located his mother's grave at Hillside Cemetery, with the help of Bill Maguire, long-time undertaker in Silverton.

The five year old boy who was placed in an orphanage, Gene Ecker (Eccher), went on to live a fulfilling, useful and happy life. At the age of 81 years, he died January 17, 1995, at his home in Hemet, California, surrounded by the love of his very large family which included his wife, Bernice, six children, and more than 50 grandchildren, great-grandchildren and great-great grandchildren. The entire family planned and participated in his beautiful Mass of the Resurrection.

**FARROW, RACHEL ELIZABETH** - First Burial in Hillside Cemetery
(17) - 1871 or 1872 - Aug 27, 1875 - Age 3 or 4 Years - Rachel was the first person to be buried at Hillside Cemetery; source of the information for Rachel is the Del Norte, Colorado, newspaper of September 4, 1875, and was furnished for this record by Allen Nossaman. A letter dated August 29, 1875, published in the Del Norte newspaper described Rachel's funeral, which took place on that date in Silverton:

"There was a funeral here today. It was that of a little girl 7 years old (she was actually 3 or 4), whose parents' name is Faro (Farrow). This is Silverton's first funeral and the first natural death in the Park (Baker's Park, later called Silverton). But human nature is the same in this wild country as in more civilized lands. A mother's heart is the same everywhere; the loss of a beloved child brings to it the same anguish; the rattle of the clods on the coffin lid fill her with the same despair among these wild mountains as it would in the most beautiful cemetery, surrounded by the most costly and beautiful monuments. The grave was made in a beautiful spot on the Howardsville road, which will probably be set aside for the cemetery. The people of the Park were very sympathetic and did everything they could to assist the bereaved family."

Rachel Elizabeth was born in Kansas, perhaps near Coffeyville where her older brother, Irven (or Irving), was born March 10, 1870. The father, Mason Farrow, was born into a family of nine brothers on November 10, 1826, in Kentucky. When a young man, he and his brother, Joe, went to Kansas to farm, and there each met his future wife. (Joe later married Hattie Miller, and Mason married her sister, Martha; their mother was a quarter Choctaw Indian.)

In 1849 Mason joined the gold rush to California, and Joe went to Texas to seek his fortune. Mason eventually returned to the midwest and it is not known where he spent the Civil War years. He and Martha Jane Miller Frasier were married in 1869, when he was 43 and she was a 29 year old widow. When she was 17 Martha married a ship captain, Daniel Frasier, and their son, Daniel, was born about 1858; the father died of yellow fever shortly thereafter, and was buried at sea.

Mason and Rachel, along with Martha's 11 year old son, Daniel, made their home near Coffeyville, Kansas, where their first child, Irven, was born in 1870; Rachel Elizabeth was born in 1871 or 1872, the parents decided to go west to the Rocky Mountains and their third child, Lucinda May, was born in Colorado in 1873. In the spring of 1875 the family started for Baker's Park (Silverton) by way of Stony Pass. The pregnant 35 year old Martha, as well as their three children, the eldest three years old, rode burros, while the 49 year old Mason and 16 year old Daniel Frasier walked.

In Silverton the family built a small cabin and on August 5, 1875, another daughter, Nevada Ann Farrow, was born. She was the second Silverton-born child. (The first child born in Silverton was Anna Silverton Taft, born July 29, 1875 a week before the birth of Nevada Ann Farrow.)

When the new baby, Nevada Ann, was three weeks old, her sister, Rachel, died of mountain fever (pneumonia). There was no established cemetery so the father went up to the second mesa or bench above town (on Boulder Mountain) and marked out a cemetery. A few burials had taken place at other county locations, but Rachel's grave in the extreme southeast corner (at that time) was the first one in what became known as Hillside Cemetery. Her marker in Sector 17, in the part of the cemetery with the earliest marked graves, was donated in 1995.

The family moved from Silverton before winter set in and lived in the lower altitude of the Animas Valley; they later moved to the Pine River Valley near Bayfield, Colorado, where they homesteaded. Other children born to Mason and Martha after they left Silverton were Rocky Mountain, Richard Valentine and Roy L. Farrow. In about 1904, Mason and Martha moved to Silver City, New Mexico; Mason died in 1907 and Martha Miller Frasier Farrow died in 1913. Both are buried at Silver City.

**GROW, "BESSIE"** - (The German name "Von Grau" was changed to "Grow" in America)

(17) - July 16, 1879 - July 28, 1881 - When she was three weeks old, little Bessie, whose full name was Elizabeth Margaret Grow, the firstborn and only child of "Doc" and Maggie, was baptized in Silverton by the parish priest, John Brinker. Sponsors for the happy occasion were Frank Schneider and Hanna Rellahan. This bright and interesting little girl was the joy and light of her home, then twelve days after her second birthday, death cruelly snatched her away. Only those who have gone through the affliction of the loss of a dear child could know the void in the aching hearts of her parents. The funeral, held at the church, was largely attended by Doc and Maggie's many friends. There were not many graves at Hillside Cemetery on that summer afternoon when the stricken parents and townspeople followed the small casket up the steep slope of Boulder Mountain. Bessie and her sister, Josie, who died about two years later, now lie in a wrought iron fenced enclosure in the aspens under a lovely white marble double tombstone, with no dates and no last name shown; merely "Bessie" on the left side and "Josie" on the right. Lettered underneath is "Our Babes".

Doc and Maggie later became the parents of eight other children. They moved to a ranch near Delta in 1885 and in the next few years moved back to Silverton for a time and also lived in Durango. In 1890 "Doc" published a notice in the Silverton newspaper, informing those who owed him money "I need money very badly. Am sick and blind and have a family to support." Described as a man of sterling quality and with a keen business ability, "Doc" died of a cerebral hemorrhage at Cory, Colorado, on March 9, 1906. He had been blind the last 12 years of his life, and received a Civil War pension of $8.00 a month.

The mother of the family, Maggie Donovan Grow, died August 14, 1913, when her buggy got stuck in the middle of a creek near Cory, Colorado; while trying to get the horses "unstuck", she overexerted herself and died.

## GROW, "JOSIE" MARY JOSEPHINE

(17) - Aug 7, 1882 - Mar 12, 1883 - Age 7 Months - Just two years previously, this little girl's sister, Bessie, firstborn of "Doc" and Maggie Grow, had died and was buried at Hillside. The arrival of this bonny baby girl about a year later, had made the young parents happy once again, but very soon, the angel of death took away their second little girl. Harlan P. Roberts, former pastor of the

Congregational Church, conducted the funeral, held at the residence, and the house was filled with sympathetic friends. The child looked lovely as she laid in the little coffin decked with choice flowers.

> *"Softly the stars are shining*
> *upon a precious grave,*
> *Beneath lie two we dearly loved*
> *but whom we could not save."*

In July 1995 nieces of Bessie and Josie Grow, Sybil Moschetti and Evelyn Helm, visited the burial site of the two little sisters who sleep forever at Hillside and arranged for repair to the plot, fence, tombstone, and an additional tombstone to give the full names of Bessie and Josie. Sybil and Evelyn were the daughters of William Grow, brother of Bessie and Josie.

**GUSTAFSON, NELS** - Shenandoah Snowslide (2) Temporary Marker near Luigi Rosa - Dec 25, 1875 - Mar 17, 1906 - Age 30 Years - Nels, a young Swedish miner in the prime of life, died on that fateful St. Patrick's Day in 1906, a date to be long remembered in the district. When the clouds lifted after a week of unbroken storms, reports of disasters began coming in thick and fast. The streets of Silverton were filled with men coming down from the mines and tales of the deadly avalanches were the sole topic of conversation. S.F. Nelson and four companions came down to town on Monday morning from the Shenandoah Mine; the other workmen remained at the mine, fearing to venture forth because of the deep snow and the very real danger of further slides. The five who did come started two slides which they narrowly escaped. They brought news of the Shenandoah Mine snowslide where twelve men lost their lives and nine others were caught but survived. One or two bodies were near the surface and could be recovered as soon as a rescue party could successfully operate, but the other bodies were scattered along the path of the slide or in the bottom of the gulch buried under a mass of snow. The body of Flake Blanton was the first one found by the search party sent to the Shenandoah Mine on the next Thursday. It was impossible to get his body to town that night, but it was brought in on Friday morning. By March 31st, six other victims had been recovered, including Nels Gustafson.

Born in Sweden, the son of A.G. Johnson and the former Mary Elizabeth Brunstrom, Nels had lived in Silverton two years, and his brother, Erick Anton Gustafson had recently come to Silverton to make his home.

A triple funeral was held Sunday, March 25th, for Nels, Peter Carlberg and Luigi Rosa (shortened from Rosadas). Carlberg was another victim of the same snowslide, and Rosa, who worked at the Silver Lake, was a victim of pneumonia. The impressive service was held at Miners Union Hall under the auspices of the Silverton Miners Union No. 26 W.F.M. Over 350 members of the union marched in the melancholy funeral procession to Hillside. All three men were buried at Hillside on that cold and snowy day; Luigi Rosa is the only one who has a tombstone.

A survivor of the slide, W.N. Hall, later described his experience, saying the snow lay heavy above the mine, but the men were not nervous. The shift boss, Addison "Ed" Kirk, one of the victims, had taken snapshots of the overhanging drifts, which a few hours later swept him into eternity (the pictures were later developed and were exceptionally good). The slide struck like a thunderbolt with no forewarning ... absolutely nothing. After supper, the men were chatting, smoking and playing checkers, with everything sociable and homelike, and the next second they were out in the snow, struggling like drowning men, swept along on top and underneath, as helpless as feathers in a whirlwind. The slide started from the summit of the mountain, 200 feet above the Shenandoah property.

When the slide came to a standstill, three men found themselves on top of the slide and frantically tried to rescue their companions, some of whom were buried a few feet under the hard packed snow, while others had parts of their heads and hands protruding from the vast whiteness. After a couple of hours of frenzied work in the dark in a blinding snowstorm, nine men were dug out, some injured from the snow and timbers of the demolished building. The survivors spent that night in the engine room in the tunnel, burning candles to keep warm. The next morning they went down into the ore house, built a fire in the stove and remained there until Monday morning. One of the men who was rescued, Harvey Bennett, was left with an enduring fear of snowslides; he and his wife, Dollie, were both killed when he tried to rescue her from another snowslide in 1916.

Those killed in the Shenandoah slide were Bert Albert, Flake Blanton, Emil Bro, Peter Carlberg, Dominic Feraglio, Nels Gustafson, Gus Heise, Addison J. "Ed" Kirk, Antonio "Tony" Oberto, Jesse Shaw, Jacob Theobald and James Vercelli. As the bodies were recovered from under the snow and debris, ten of the twelve victims were buried at Hillside and two were buried elsewhere: Addison Kirk at Grand Junction, Colorado, and Jesse Shaw at Shawnee, Oklahoma.

There were numerous snowslides in the county that March 17, 1906, snuffing out the lives of 21 men altogether, and injuring many others. August Bessee and "Steamshovel John" Zanei were standing on the dump of the Big Colorado Mine, along with a mule and five cars of ore when a slide swept them down the mountain 600 feet. The men were dug out, not too seriously injured. The mule was killed. Bessee, whose foot was crushed, was pulled from Silverton down the canyon to Elk Park on a sled, then went by train to Trimble Springs to recuperate. He credited the saving of his life to his dog, a common cur. When his master was carried down the mountain by the avalanche of snow, the dog followed, quickly located him then began to frantically dig the snow away from him. Because the dog succeeded in uncovering Bessee's face, he was given a chance to breathe until rescued.

In other fatal slides of March 17, 1906, two men, George Abbott and Lucky Bill Thompson, were killed at Burro Bridge

(Bonner Mine); at the Silver Wing bunk house near Animas Forks, it was George Marcott who was killed; and at the Sunlight bunk house, also near Animas Forks, Joe Walker met death; at the prophetically named Last Chance Mine (Unity Tunnel), Rudolph Paveglio was taken; and at the Green Mountain property in Cunningham Gulch, D.R. Hickey suddenly entered eternity. The loss of life that day was truly appalling.

## HACKETT, TOM

No Marker - Died Apr 25, 1895 - Age 45 Years - A very competent and widely known mining man, Tom had been in charge of some of the largest mines in southwestern Colorado. He was born in Ireland and came to the Silverton mining area in the late 1870s, where he proved himself to be a hard working, law abiding citizen. By his industry and economy he had accumulated some property.

Tom and Lucy Higgins, daughter of Tom P. Higgins and his first wife, were married in Silverton on Sunday, December 28, 1884, at the residence of her father and his second wife. The ceremony was performed by Rev. Father Ley in the presence of a small number of intimate friends. William Sullivan was best man and Miss Mary Weddell was bridesmaid.

The bride was most becomingly attired in a very handsome brocaded blue silk costume and diamond ornaments.

Children born to Tom and Lucy were sons, Francis D. (Frank), in 1885, Thomas B. in 1890, Arthur J. in 1893, and daughter, Claire Agnes, in 1894.

In an unfortunate, nearly fatal 1891 mine accident, Tom had a very narrow escape from death, and the resulting injuries were felt to be directly responsible for his death four years later. As superintendent of the North Star on King Solomon Mountain, Tom was working in one of the drifts when at least a ton of rock slab fell on him, hitting him between the shoulders and on his head. He was knocked unconscious and was severely crushed in his chest and head. Dr. Brown hoped to have him fit for duty in about ten days! He did live to return to work, but was definitely somewhat incapacitated.

In March 1895 the newspaper reported "Poor Tom Hackett!! On Wednesday they brought him home from the mountain, a raving maniac! Oh, the pity of it! Reason gone, hope lost, life blighted!"

A jury was empaneled that same day, and Tom was adjudged to be insane. It was widely believed the ton of rock which hit him in the head four years previously had caused his insanity. The newspaper noted there was no hope of his recovery, and if that were so, it would be better for Tom if they put him on the hill in the city of the dead (the cemetery). Sheriff Hank Sherman, by himself, took Hackett to the insane asylum at Pueblo the next day, and Tom, a strong and powerful man, was very violent at times during the trip.

Less than a month after being confined to the insane asylum, Tom Hackett did die. (Several instances were found where those sent to the insane asylum died soon after being committed.)

Tom's remains were returned to Silverton and his funeral was held at St. Patrick Church, with burial at Hillside. Survivors were his wife and their young children, Frank, Tom, Art, and the baby girl, Claire, only eight months old. Although not named in Tom's obituary, his sister, Jane Hackett (Mrs. Con Callahan) of Silverton, also survived. In addition to his family, Tom left a large circle of old friends to mourn his tragic demise.

Tom's widow, Lucy Higgins Hackett, married Thomas G. Edwards at the Palace Hotel in Durango on January 1, 1900. Children born to them were George, James and Gertrude Frances. Tom Edwards was a building contractor who built several Silverton buildings, including the Wyman, Curtis Hardware and Johnny's Cash Store. In 1902 he was awarded the contract for Silverton's new brick jail, which was located between Reese and Greene Streets, above 15th Street. Tom Edwards also met a tragic and violent death; he was killed in a 1909 Minnie Gulch excavation cave-in. He, too, is buried at Hillside. Lucy Higgins Hackett Edwards died in Los Angeles, California, in 1934 at the home of her daughter, Claire (Mrs. Vernon Drury).

**HOVEY, BURKE** - Died 1885 - Snowslide - Son of Aaron Hovey
No Marker - Died Dec 22, 1885 - Age 20 Years - Burke, referred to as the nephew of Miles Frank Hovey of Silverton, had only recently arrived from New Brunswick, Canada. He left Silverton with J.M. Skates to work at the Prodigal Son Mine, about four miles up Cement Creek. They entered the mine shaft on December 22nd and were never again seen alive.

A very wet snow had fallen and some kind of slight disturbance set off a huge avalanche which buried the two men inside the mine. They were 90 feet below the surface of the ground under 25 feet of snow and ice. Soon several men from nearby dug through the tightly packed snow and ice and came upon an extended hand, still warm, but both men were dead. One was probably killed by falling against the wall of the shaft and the other smothered to death while trying to dig his way out from the imprisoning snow.

The bodies of the two victims were brought to town, suitably cared for by relatives and friends, and laid out in citizens clothes of black. Handsome coffins were procured and everything done which a universal feeling of respect and sorrow could demand. The double funeral was held at the Congregational Church the day before Christmas. Then the bodies were pulled by sled to the cemetery where the deep snow had been cleared away in order to dig the graves. The procession following the dead men to their final resting place was one of the largest ever witnessed in the San Juan.

The family of Aaron Hovey and his wife consisted of nine children, and Burke was the first member of the family to live on the western slope of Colorado. He first came to Colorado in 1883 and lost his life before other family members arrived. His brother, Frank Hovey, became the sheriff at Montrose, Colorado, and his sister, Mina, married Liberty C. Heath, a pioneer resident of the Uncompahgre Valley; Mina died in Oakland, California, in July 1943. Another sister, Lizzie Hovey Phelps, remained in Canada.

## KING, DAVID "B.O. PLENTY"
(1) - Mar 3, 1883 - Jan 1, 1960 - The year of birth lettered on his marker is 1873; his obituary cited 1883. Dave was found frozen and dead in his tar paper shack on Cement Street. Excess alcohol was said to have caused his death. After not having seen Dave for several days, Frank "Corky" Scheer checked on him and found his body.

With his beard and walking stick, Dave had looked the part of an old time Silverton prospector, which he was not, but sometimes claimed to be. His obituary and another article, both written by Larry Beaber, noted King had earned the nickname of "B.O. Plenty" because of his total lack of personal hygiene. (B.O. Plenty was a character in the *Dick Tracy* comic strip.) When found on New Years Day, his shack was a sickening and filthy sight, a place where others would be ashamed to keep pigs. A dirty old pillow was stuffed in a broken window; his bed, an old broken down army cot, was held up by an old overturned tub; the mattress was blackened by years of dirt and soil, the stuffing exposed and strewn over the floor. He had frozen to death in a kneeling position, no coat, and wearing his only pair of filthy overalls. There was little else in the foul and squalid room. A frozen water line came up through the floor; a cracked pot-bellied stove was thick with ashes; the walls of the small room where he existed were black with years of smoke and dirt; a solitary shelf held an empty coffee can; there were no dishes and the only visible utensil was a meat skewer with dried food caked thickly to it. There were a couple of dented dirty pans on the floor which was littered with empty wine bottles, human excrement and ashes. Here he had lived and here he had died.

"B.O." had received a monthly old age pension check, but persisted in spending any money he had on booze. A guardian was appointed to see that he had food and coal, and Dave would usually trade the food for wine. Time and time again the welfare director would furnish him blankets and encourage him to live like a human being, but it did absolutely no good.

Neither did the suggestion of a rest home. Furniture, even a radio, were given to him, which he chopped into kindling wood. He asked favors of no one and lived to himself, for himself. Dave, born in Kansas, had once lived in Wichita. No one knew why he came to Silverton in 1945. For several years he had hauled garbage and ashes in an old dilapidated wagon, pulled by a poor old skinny horse. "B.O." would often get drunk and tie the horse outside his shack, completely neglecting to feed him. At least one of his animals died of starvation. It was difficult to imagine and impossible to understand why he lived as he did. It was so bad he was even asked to give his grocery order from outside the store because the stench of his body was so strong it was impossible for anyone to stay in the same room with him.

"B.O." was buried at Hillside Cemetery and a graveside prayer was offered for him. If he had a reason to live as he did, B.O. carried that reason with him to the grave.

**KINNEY, MABEL L.** - Scarlet Fever, Meningitis
(21) - Jan 14, 1894 - Feb 1, 1900 - Age 6 Years  This darling adored child of a lifetime lived but a brief time on earth; the thin thread

of her life was broken after a severe illness with scarlet fever and tubercular meningitis. She had been ill 24 days and all through her sickness she bore her sufferings bravely, for she possessed remarkable fortitude for one so young. For a time prior to death, Mabel's feeble pulse appeared to grow stronger, and her parents' hearts beat wildly with hope; then came the change, and blighted hope, mingled with soul-wrenching grief, reposed over the child's dead form.

A winsome little girl, Mabel was very nearly idolized by all. None who knew her failed to recognize the beauty of her nature and love her for her sweet simplicity. Her funeral was held from the Kinney residence on upper Greene Street, with Rev. George Eaves officiating. She was buried at Hillside, near the top of the cemetery in a plot which was later fenced with wrought iron.

> *"and she lies quietly sleeping*
> *in the shadow of the pines."*

(from a poem written for Mabel's mother by a friend)

Mabel's adoptive father, Willis Z. Kinney was born in 1860 in the state of New York. He lived on a farm until 1880 when he went to work in a smelter in Pueblo, Colorado. He prospected around Silver Cliff, Colorado, a couple of years then came to the Silverton area in 1883. An early San Juaner, he packed his blankets up Cement Creek searching for the treasures hidden in the mountains. He existed on salt side, bread, ambition and hope. In about 1893 he was hired by investors Cyrus W. Davis of Waterville, Maine, and Henry M. Soule of Boston, Massachusetts, to manage their properties. In 1894 the men bought the Gold King Mine for $15,000 from Louise Erickson Nelson Forsyth, the widow of Olaf Arvid Nelson, who discovered and worked on the early development of the Gold King. Davis and Soule put up the money for the purchase, and Willis Kinney contributed his time and expertise in developing the property. The venture was very successful and in 1900 when Mabel died, the capital stock of the company was $6,000,000.00 and no shares were for sale.

In September of 1887, Willis Kinney and Miss Mary Wirtzenberger of Denver, formerly of Blue Lick Springs, Kentucky, were married in Durango. For several years, the couple spent their winters isolated at their mining property in Porcupine Gulch, coming down to Silverton only rarely. Mary Kinney became quite expert at skiing.

Sometime after Mabel's birth in 1894, probably in Denver, she was adopted by Willis and Mary Kinney. In April 1899, after the Kinneys became rather well off, they were involved in a court case in Denver and the natural mother of the child (Mrs. Becktloff, formerly Briton), succeeded in having five year old Mabel taken away from the Kinneys. Willis Kinney telegraphed a friend in Silverton, "Our little Mabel is taken from us and my wife is broken-hearted".

In September of 1899, six months after Mabel was taken from them, Mary and Willis Kinney and little Mabel, "the child whose ownership was tried in the Denver court last winter", returned to Silverton. Mabel was once again the happy adopted daughter of the Kinneys and their joy was boundless. Then only four months later, this precious little girl, who had brought the greatest happiness into the lives of her adopted parents, died in the cold Silverton winter.

In March, a month after Mabel's death, Willis and Mary Kinney returned from Denver accompanied by a bright-eyed little miss of seven years, who was to be their new adopted daughter. With their grief still fresh from losing their Mabel, Mary Kinney named her new little girl Helen Mabel Kinney. About three weeks later, in April 1900, for reasons unknown, Mrs. Kinney took Helen Mabel back to Denver and exchanged her for another little girl, whose name and age are not known. They returned to Silverton about the middle of April and about three months later, in July 1900, Mrs. Kinney and her new daughter visited Mrs. Kinney's former home in Blue Lick Springs, Kentucky. If that little girl ever came back to Silverton, there was no mention of it in the newspapers.

In January 1901, Mrs. Kinney again returned from Denver, this time bringing two little girls, ages ten weeks and one year. Hiram and Flora Nichols Washburn adopted the older child, naming her Mary Willis Washburn (the first names of their friends, Willis and Mary Kinney); Willis and Mary Kinney adopted the younger baby, naming her Gertrude Mary, and they kept this little girl. In November 1903 the newspaper reported that Willis and Mary Kinney had adopted a little boy a little over two years old who was too young to appreciate the good fortune that was his. The boy and his nurse were in Silverton while Mrs. Kinney and Gertrude had gone on a California trip. The lucky little boy was not mentioned again. In 1905 Mrs. Kinney and Gertrude moved permanently to 745 Corona in Denver, and Willis Kinney spent most of his time in Silverton, and often visited his wife and daughter in Denver. Gertrude Mary grew up, attended North Side High School where she was a freshman in May 1914, and rarely visited Silverton. Mary Wirtzenberger Kinney died in 1930, and Willis Z. Kinney died in 1934, both in Denver, and both are buried there at Crown Hill Cemetery.

Mary Willis Washburn, the little year old girl adopted by Hiram and Flora Washburn at the same time Gertrude was adopted by the Kinneys, married Lester Francis Sumner on September 19, 1919, in Pueblo, Colorado. They moved to Portland, Oregon, in 1921, where Mr. Sumner died in 1946. Mary remained there until 1977, when she moved to Tampa, Florida, to live with her son, Robert S. Sumner; she died there in 1978. Robert S. Sumner, her son, was born in Portland, Oregon, November 15, 1921, and in 1987 lived in Tampa, Florida. He found the name of his mother's natural mother to be Jenny Woodward.

## LEVEQUE, LOUIS, MRS.
No Marker - Died Aug 29, 1895 - A shocking and ghastly accident occurred near the power

station, and the deplorable side of the sad occurrence was the fact that Louis Leveque, his wife and two friends, were in a sad state of intoxication, nothing unusual for them.

The party of four had hired a team and carriage in Silverton to take them to Howardsville where they overindulged in intoxicants. When they started for home their conditions were such that they would have made a good example for a temperance lecturer. Later, when Leveque had sufficiently recovered from his inebriety to coherently relate the circumstances, he stated he and his wife were thrown over the dashboard of their carriage while making the descent from the county road to the toll road near the electric power plant. With the horses on a dead run down the steep incline, one of the reins slipped from Leveque's hands and in trying to regain it, he fell over the dashboard and was run over by the carriage. His wife then endeavored to recover the reins and she fell over the dashboard, catching her left leg in the spokes of the wheel, severing it at the knee joint with no attachment left but a slight piece of skin. She also suffered severe internal injuries. They were brought to Silverton for medical aid, but Mrs. Leveque was too weak to undergo an amputation, and it was a foregone conclusion she would not survive. She passed to the seat of judgment a little after midnight.

Her funeral was held the next day at the Congregational church and she was buried at Hillside Cemetery, on the side of Boulder Mountain. Although badly injured, her husband recovered, but as noted in the newspaper, *"the recklessness of reckless characters often brings their doom! But then*
... *"Touch her not scornfully!*
*Think of her mournfully!*
*Gently and humanly, Not of the stains of her.*
*All that remains of her,*
*Now is pure womanly.*
*Make no deep scrutiny, into her mutiny,*
*Rash and undutiful, past all dishonor,*
*Death has left on her, only the beautiful."*

**LEWIS, CARRIE FRANCES CLARK DAVIS** - Snowslide
(19) - Dec 21, 1865 - Mar 11, 1911 - Age 45 Years - The tranquility of the day gave no indication that the grim reaper was about to visit and gather in Carrie Lewis and her granddaughter, baby Carrie Schnee, along with Laura Fay True and Samson Hore. At 11:00 o'clock on that long ago Saturday morning, 45 year old Carrie Lewis was preparing noon dinner at the Gold King Mine boarding house

on Bonita Mountain, where she had been working as cook for seven months. Her eleven months old granddaughter, little Carrie Schnee, was playing on the floor with childish delight. Without a moment's warning the crash came and there was barely time for them to look at each other before heaven and earth gave away and the huge building was crushed to kindling wood by the gigantic snowslide. Carrie and her little granddaughter were swept into eternity, as were Laura Fay True and Samson Hore. Laura's husband, M.O. True, was trapped alive under the tightly packed snow. Laura and her husband had both been in the kitchen with Carrie Lewis and the baby, while Samson Hore had been in the upper part of the boarding house.

The slide was a very peculiar one. It covered an area three fourths of a mile wide and started high on Bonita Peak, running over half a mile through timber without destroying the trees. Then it hit the huge new boarding house, less than two years old, and from there to the bottom of the gulch cleared away everything before it. From the way in which debris was scattered about it appeared that slides had come from different directions and crossed paths. The snow in places was over 50 feet deep, packed very solidly.

At about 3:00 that afternoon, Charles Airy, who was working in Gladstone, looked up toward the mine and thought it looked as if a slide had run; he and Ike Camp immediately made their way up the mountain through the snow until they came in sight of the awesome tragedy. They hailed the men remaining at Gladstone, who rushed to the scene and all proceeded to do what was possible for the victims. They heard M.O. True's faint voice from his icy living grave, and digging like mad men succeeded in getting him out, still alive. He had been buried under 15 feet of snow for eight hours, expecting each moment to be his last. Although he had no bones broken, his entire body, including his head, was one mass of bruises. Only the strongest constitution and soundest mind could have endured the hours of his imprisonment in the dark and frigid death trap.

Owing to difficulties in getting word to Silverton it was after 11:00 that night when news of the disaster was received in town. Immediately County Coroner R.E. McLeod, H.A. Allen and two others, made preparation for the hazardous trip nine miles up the canyon through the deep and treacherous snow. They reached the scene of the disaster at 3:45 the next morning (Sunday) after a long, hard and perilous trip. Upon arrival they learned the bodies of Laura True, Carrie Lewis and little Carrie Frances Schnee had been recovered; Mr. True had been rescued and everything possible was being done for the injured man. His escape from instant death in the slide, then his rescue from underneath the snow, ice and debris, was truly miraculous.

The search continued until after sunrise for the remaining victim, Samson Hore, but without result. Since he had been in the upper story of the building when it was hit, it was expected his body had been carried down the gulch, while the others had been in the kitchen at the time of the disaster and consequently were not taken so far away.

Much sympathy was felt for Frances Schnee, daughter of Carrie Lewis and mother of the baby girl, Carrie Frances Schnee, who lacked a month of being one year old. Frances Schnee had been employed, along with her mother, at the Gold King boarding house up until the time most of the men were laid off a few weeks previously. She then went to Silverton to look for work, leaving her little daughter with her grandmother at the mine, little imagining that it would be the last time she would ever see them alive. The little girl was bright and happy, a favorite with all the men employed at the mine, each day waving her little hand to one and all as they went to and from their work, the little hand now stilled by death. Scarcely a half hour before the death dealing slide struck, Frances Schnee in Silverton had been talking over the phone to her mother and little girl. When word was brought to her a few hours later that both were dead, her grief was inconsolable. The poor young mother was heartbroken over the loss of the two so near and dear to her.

About 45 men from Silverton went to Gladstone on Sunday to lend what assistance they could. Those volunteers loaded the bodies of Carrie Lewis and Laura True on toboggans, while James Duncan tenderly carried the tiny body of Carrie Frances Schnee the nine miles through the deep snow to Prosser Undertaking in Silverton.

Mrs. Whitmore Taylor and another Mrs. Taylor who lived at the Henrietta Switch, a station of the Animas Power Company between Silverton and Gladstone, stayed up all night Saturday and Sunday, making coffee and serving food to the men making the trip to and from the slide. Mrs. C.W. Airy did much in the same capacity at Gladstone.

Carrie Lewis was born in Missouri, the daughter of Robert Clark who was born in Kentucky. She had lived in Montana and was married to a man named Davis when her daughter, Frances, was born. Carrie had come to Silverton the previous September with her daughter, Frances, and her granddaughter Carrie, who was born in Durango.

On a cold Wednesday morning, March 15, 1911, the funeral for Carrie and her granddaughter was held at the Prosser Chapel, Rev. A.W. Pink of the Congregational Church officiating. Music for the sorrowful and touching occasion was furnished by a choir composed of Delia, Carrie and George Bausman and John Hughes. The remains of the grandmother and little granddaughter were placed in the same casket, the baby lying in the arms of her grandmother. The service was very largely attended and a number of beautiful floral offerings decorated the casket. The baby's father, Edward Schnee, came up from the Animas Valley to attend the service. Many townspeople, as well as members of the Miners Union and of the Cooks and Waiters Union accompanied the remains to their last resting place at Hillside, under the deep snow. May they together sleep in eternal peace. Their tombstone was donated in 1993.

The other two snowslide victims, Laura Fay True and Samson Hore, were not buried at Hillside. Laura Fay and M.O. True, a young couple in the prime of life had been married a little over a year, and had been operating the Gold King Commissary a little more than a month. Laura was born in Kansas May 4, 1881, daughter of Newson and Mary Williams Fulton, and had lived in Colorado about 15 years. Her brother, L.F. Fulton, came from Rifle, Colorado, and accompanied Laura's body to Crawford for burial there. Paul Giers of Denver, in whose home Laura and M.O. True were married, came to Silverton to help Laura's injured husband.

The body of Samson Hore was recovered from the appalling wreckage on March 17 at 9:25 a.m. after a continuous search of six days and nights. The body had been carried over 300 feet down the gulch and was covered by three room partitions and more than twelve feet of snow. The unfortunate man was lying on his left side with his head against a typewriter which had been in the room with him. ، His skull was fractured and he had a large bruise over the kidney. Indications were that he had been in his room preparing to go down to dinner when the slide struck the building. He had removed one overshoe and the other was unbuckled; his hat and coat had been hung on the wall and when found were still hanging on the pegs. The rescue party that so diligently kept up the search for Hore included George Becker, Ike Camp, Lewis Decker, Charles Airy, Frank Oppenheiger, Lucas Aebi, J. Paul, W. Taylor, Charles Gustafson and others. The men went to work in the slide every morning at 2:00 a.m. and worked without ceasing until the afternoon sun made the danger so great that it would have been absolute folly to remain longer in the path of death. As it was, they were in constant peril and enough praise could never be given for the work done and the dangers overcome in searching for the remains of their friend. The men would work away for hours at a time and become so completely exhausted they could work no longer, then some piece of evidence would be discovered and they would go to work again with renewed vigor and further exert themselves. At last their efforts proved fruitful and Samson Hore was recovered from his snowy grave.

The men took the body as far as the Yukon Mine where they were met by a contingent of Masons who took the body the rest of the way to Silverton. Samson was placed in a casket at Prosser Undertaking Parlor, then removed to the Masonic Hall where the remains were viewed by his many acquaintances and friends. James Hore, brother of Samson, arrived on Sunday from Goldfield, Colorado, and on Monday at the noon hour the Masonic Lodge held services at their hall, after which they marched in a body to the depot, accompanying the remains. Samson was buried in Denver on the next Thursday afternoon. He was born in Cornwall, the son of William and Harriet Grose Hore, and had lived in Colorado fifteen years. He had been working at the Gold King a year as a shift boss and was survived by his mother in Cornwall and his brother in Goldfield, Colorado.

**LEWIS, NETTIE** - Suicide by Poison
No Marker - Died July 14, 1889 - A sad case of suicide by poisoning occurred at Minnie Strong's place on a Sunday night. Nettie Lewis had come to Silverton a few weeks previously from Denver and at once entered a Blair Street bagnio (brothel), but as she was "not a good rustler and too much of a lady", she was fired. She then went to Minnie Strong's, where no beer was sold, and there she appeared to be quite content.

Shortly before her suicide, Nettie took a small tin pail and went out for some beer. When she returned, she gave some of the beer to her boss, Minnie Strong, then went to her room where a male customer was waiting and they both began to drink. Nettie confessed to her male friend that she was "stuck" on him, and implored him to make her his own, then the two of them could leave Silverton and start a new life. Receiving no encouragement for her plan, Nettie quietly decided to end her life, walked to her trunk and removed a small bottle of carbolic acid. She put it to her lips and drank. Her companion snatched the bottle from her, laid her on the bed and ran downstairs to give the alarm. Dr. Pascoe was at once summoned and did all that could be done, but to no avail. Nettie died in a few moments and ended her career of shame.

A slim brunette with a pair of hands as perfect as nature ever made, Nettie had a ladylike manner about her and showed evidences of having been well raised. She had confided to a friend that she was raised in Brooklyn, New York and lived on Washington Avenue. Nettie was decently buried at Hillside after a few words and prayer at the house by Rev. J.W. King. A goodly number of her associates followed her remains to the silent city on the mountainside. *"She is at rest, touched by the magic wand of death."*

## LONERGAN, MARY ANN MCCARTHY
(Mrs. Maurice T. Lonergan)
(4) - No Marker - May 1865 - Sept 10, 1922 - Age 57 Years - After a lingering illness, Mary Ann died at the home of her sister-in-law, Miss Eliza Lonergan (who died a month later). Her illness had been greatly intensified by the mental suffering inflicted by the unexplained disappearance of her only child, Willie, sometimes referred to by family members as "Black Will" or "Willie the Black".

Mary Ann, born in Ireland, came to America in the early 1870s, and in 1882 came to Silverton with her sister, Catherine, and Catherine's husband, John Lonergan. On August 27, 1884, Mary and Maurice T. Lonergan, a brother of her sister's husband, were married in Silverton by Rev. Edmund Ley, a Catholic priest, with John O'Brien and Hanna Hayes as witnesses. At that time, Mary was 20 years old and Maurice was 35. Their only child, William, was born in September 1885. The couple apparently separated, and in the 1900 census, Mary was listed as head of the house, and her son, William, age 14, lived with her. Her husband, Maurice "Uncle Daddy" Lonergan, a saloon keeper, lived with the family of his sister, Nora Lonergan Coughlin. Maurice T. Lonergan was called

"Uncle Daddy" to distinguish him from his cousin in the area, Maurice P. Lonergan. Maurice T. "Uncle Daddy", the husband of Mary, was described as small and feisty with a long red floor length beard which he folded under his vest. Also known as "The Dublin Rooster" to many of his customers, he died in 1905 and is buried at Hillside.

Mary was survived by a large circle of friends, and her funeral was held at St. Patrick Catholic Church, conducted by Father W.B. Mayer. Her remains were laid to rest at Hillside Cemetery, borne there by William Sullivan, William Palmquist, George Landry, Mike Butler, "Will the Marshal" Lonergan, and Billy Cole, all old time friends. Sweet rest be thine, Mary.

Mary's life seems to have been permeated with sorrow and unhappiness. As recalled by Silverton native, Louie Dalla, "Black Willie" lived with his mother, who received a pension of $12.00 a month from the county. Mary loved Willie, although he drank too much and couldn't hold a job. They were poor and to stay warm in the cold winters he slept between two mattresses. At that time, undesirable characters were sometimes escorted out of town by the authorities and instructed not to return. During a siege of severely cold weather in February 1922, Charlie Leonard, the town cop, ran 36 year old Willie out of town, down the railroad track into the awesome Animas Canyon. The temperature was 37 degrees below zero and "Black Willie" was wearing only a blue serge suit and oxfords with no coat or overshoes. At the end of February, his distraught mother published a beseeching notice in the newspaper, *"Should any reader know of the whereabouts of Willie Lonergan, they will do me a favor to let me know when and where he was seen by them. He has been away from home several weeks. Address me at Silverton, Colorado."* No word was received and "Black Willie" was never heard from again.

Shortly after Willie disappeared, an unidentified man burned to death in the depot at Tefft Siding on the Denver & Rio Grande Railroad, several miles below Silverton in the rugged Animas Canyon. The building was completely destroyed by a fire of unknown origin and a search of the debris revealed the charred trunk of a human body, metal parts of clothing and the remains of a pair of oxfords. Speculations were rife in Silverton and Durango as to the probable identity of that person, and many believed the unfortunate fire victim was "Black Willie" Lonergan. The remains were taken to Durango for burial by Coroner Damon of La Plata County.

**McCARTHY, CALLAHAN** - Exposure and Freezing on Sultan Mountain
(1) - 1854 - Dec 23, 1884 - Age 30 Years - Cal, a splendid looking specimen of manhood, was born in County Cork, Ireland, and had come to Silverton in 1882 to join his brother, Eugene McCarthy. On December 8th, although the skies looked stormy, Cal left town to look for a lost horse on Sultan Mountain, accompanied by John Lonergan of the Railroad Hotel, and Joe Reynolds. The men expected to return in about two days. Lonergan and Reynolds were on horseback and carried the matches, food and other supplies; Cal was on foot and carried a breech loading shotgun in case he saw any game, but no matches or food. The men agreed they would meet at the Molas Mine, about four miles up the mountain from town, and if they didn't connect there, would meet at Hershie's cabin near the lake, then search for the horse. When McCarthy reached the mine at about 3:00 in the afternoon, he learned Lonergan and Reynolds had gone on, so he continued onward in spite of the threatening weather, expecting to find them in camp near the lake. A very heavy and

severe San Juan blizzard descended upon the mountain with a fury, and Cal stumbled along and made his way as best he could, but finally, blinded by the snow and exhausted from fighting against the wind, became bewildered and completely lost the trail.

He struggled on and on and as darkness fell, discovered he had been traveling in a circle, making no headway at all. He knew death would overtake him unless he kept moving, and during the greater portion of that night, he was able to stay in motion. He would stop at intervals, remove his boots and rub his feet with snow to keep them from freezing. The weather grew increasingly colder and his sufferings on the next day were extremely intense. He was also very hungry, and succeeded in killing a rabbit, which he ate raw, as there was no hope of making a fire. Through that entire day and night, then the next two endless days and nights, Cal continued wandering aimlessly about, trying to keep from freezing to death. Finally, his strength completely exhausted, and overcome with hunger, he gave up and sank down upon a fallen tree. Feeling there was no hope, he submitted to inevitable death.

Messrs. Brewster and Bats from Silverton had

gone out hunting on Saturday morning, saw a man's tracks in the snow, and knowing of McCarthy's being lost, followed the tracks and found Cal on the mountain between the Aletha and Molas mines; they took him about a mile and a half to the Aletha Mine buildings, fed him and made him as comfortable as possible and sent word to Silverton of his rescue. Eugene McCarthy, Cal's brother, was overjoyed to learn his brother had been found, still alive. He and several friends had been searching for Cal every day without success, and Eugene was at the depot about to take the train to Rockwood, then return on the old trail back to Silverton, to again look for his brother that day. With joy unbounded, Eugene, along with Billy Koehler, Maurice Lonergan, John Steidelman and William Mulatti got horses and went to the Aletha Mine where the suffering man was put upon a horse and brought back to Silverton. More dead than alive, delirious, his hands and feet frozen solid, Cal was in very bad condition; however, Dr. Jim Brown prescribed remedies and gave the patient close attention and thought Cal was doing well enough he might escape having to undergo any amputations. Callahan's comrades, John Lonergan and Joe Reynolds, did not return to Silverton until after Cal's safe return to town, and they had supposed he had long before returned or had stayed at one of the mines; they knew nothing of his hazardous experience on the mountain.

Contrary to Dr. Brown's hopeful expectations, and after suffering untold agonies, poor Cal McCarthy died ten days after his rescue from the mountain. The funeral was attended by a large number of Silverton's best known citizens, and he was buried at Hillside on the day before Christmas, during another San Juan storm. His brother, Eugene, and Eugene's little girl, Cora, were later buried beside him. The marker for Cal was donated in 1986.

Many years later, in 1917, John Lonergan, one of the men Cal was to meet at the Molas Mine, met a remarkably similar fate; he is also buried at Hillside.

**McENAY, PETER** - Gold King Fire
(2) Temporary Marker - Died June 6, 1908 - Age 50 Years - Peter, a member of the rescue party, died after the disastrous fire at the Gold King Mine, He had been in the Silverton area about five months, having come from Butte, Montana. He was a widower with a 19 year old son, Thomas J. McEnay, working in the mines at Butte, Montana, and another son and two daughters in the State Orphans' Home.

A pall of the deepest gloom enshrouded Silverton on Friday night, June 5th, when the catastrophic news was telephoned to Silverton from Gladstone that the Gold King Mine buildings above Gladstone, high on the slope of Bonita Mountain, were on fire. The Gold King Mill in Gladstone was connected to the mine by a long aerial tramway, and the operation employed about 200 men. At the time of the disaster the second shift was underground working in the mine.

Ed McKay, mine foreman, directed shift bosses Peter McEnay and Roy Coburn to get the men out of the mine immediately, which they did, to the great relief of all. Carbonic gas and smoke pouring into the mine, poisoning the air, could have killed everyone in the mine. (Two months later, mine foreman Ed McKay, unable to recover from the tragic loss of six fellow workers in this monumental disaster, also died and is buried at Hillside.)

It was soon apparent there was no way to check the ravages of the all-consuming fire, and every building in its path was destroyed ... the four story boarding house, stables, shops, storage buildings and offices. Those in the boarding house escaped injury except for Henry Fitzgee, who jumped from a fourth floor window and hurt his back; he later recovered.

After the fire burned out most of those from the mine and boarding house went down to Silverton. There they talked of the fire, gathered in the saloons, found places to sleep and tried to figure out what to do, as they were now unemployed. Most of the men lost their personal belongings and money in the blaze. The Gold King suffered a loss close to $100,000, although they had about $40,000 worth of insurance. Fred C. Grebles, operator of the boarding house, suffered a loss of several thousand dollars, and had no insurance. The fire had been a serious disaster, but everyone was thankful that no lives had been lost. That feeling would soon turn to panic, then horror.

The next morning, Saturday, word spread that no one had seen three of the miners who had been working in the mine at the time of the fire ... Victor Erickson, his brother-in-law, Otto Johnson, and John Fenstrom (or Finstrom). Superintendent Willis Z. Kinney was at Gladstone and could not be reached because the telephone wire was down. When he arrived in Silverton at noon and learned of the fear that three men were still in the mine, he made hurried arrangements for a special train to take men and supplies to Gladstone (about nine miles) to rescue the three men from their deadly predicament.

Kinney and Peter McEnay, shift boss, then secured a light engine and raced up the railroad track as fast as possible to Gladstone. McEnay was overcome with grief at the idea that any men were left in the mine, as he had been confident all were out. At Gladstone, Kinney and McEnay were joined by Alfred W. Burns and others of the mill force, and the men climbed the steep mountain to the portal above the second level of the mine. (The aerial tram had been destroyed by the fire.) Already exhausted by the climb up the steep mountain, 48 year old Willis Kinney, 50 year old Peter McEnay and 26 year old Alfred Burns, went down into the gas and smoke filled mine. Burns, who worked at the mill, had previously worked in the mine and knew his way around.

The further down they went, the worse the air became, and at the second level Kinney was almost completely overcome. He had to climb the ladders back out to fresh air, which took him an hour and a half. McEnay and Burns, although suffering intensely, continued on down to levels three and four; at level four

Burns was unable to go on, but McEnay struggled on down to level five, where the three missing men had been working. He found them all alive and yelled up the shaft telling Willis Kinney the men were found. Kinney, by that time, was almost prostrated from the effects of the carbonic acid gas, and believing all was well with the men in the mine, returned to Silverton.

McEnay, Erickson, Fenstrom and Johnson started the long strenuous climb back up the ladders which led out of the mine. They reached the fourth level and found Burns unconscious, but overcome by smoke and gases themselves, they were too weak to help him and in their helpless condition, simply laid down and went to sleep. As described by a survivor of the disaster, the gas gave a peculiar sensation as it slowly overcame a person ... "There was no sensation sweeter or more peaceful. All I cared to do was to lie down and be let alone. I was perfectly happy and desired only to be permitted to sleep. The sensation was delightful and I did not realize that it was the sleep of death that was stealing over me."

In the meantime, another thirty men left Silverton on still another special train in the early afternoon. Included in that number were Roy Coburn, Gus Olson and Alex Johnson, none of whom returned alive. Upon arriving in Gladstone the rescuers headed down into the mine, led by Roy Coburn and Martin Duggan, who were familiar with the mine. They found all the men alive and attempts were made to take out the men who had been there the longest; however, once again the rescuers themselves were soon overcome by the poisonous air, and one by one they passed out in the mine tunnels or wandered about helplessly, dazed and disoriented. The electric hoist was not operating, the power having been cut off by the fire, and there was no way to take the men to the surface except to carry them. Some of the stronger men carried out the sick and unconscious, and cases of individual heroism were without number. The bravery of the men who continued to re-enter the mine in an endeavor to rescue the stricken ones, could not be described or measured.

Peter McEnay and Al Burns, the first who entered, were found unconscious by Thad McLean and placed on a mine car to be pushed out to the shaft. When Thad started to push the car, he found a body on the track and was too weak to lift it off so the car could pass. The bodies of McEnay and Burns, cold in death, were later found in the mine car by one of the last rescue parties. Many of the men were carried out from levels two and three after succumbing to the gas, but it was impossible to get the men from level four, deeper in the mine. Gloom settled down on the sick and fatigued band of heroic workers.

Another rescue train with a hundred willing workers left Silverton at 10:00 o'clock Saturday night. By the time they arrived in Gladstone, connections had been made with the electric lines and the hoist was started. Lew Haas, Theodore Boak and Alex Bausman headed the search in a systematic manner. As fast as the hoist brought a load of disabled and dead to the surface the brave workers went back for others. Each level of the mine was searched until 7:00 o'clock the next morning when both the dead and the living had all been taken out of the mine. The last to be found were Herman Matson, the most seriously injured man to survive (but who was never a well man again), and the dead bodies of Roy Coburn and August Olson (Oleson).

The train from Gladstone bearing six dead bodies and three score sick and disabled men, reached Silverton at about 9:00 on Sunday morning. It was a ghastly and horrible sight.

The dead were (1)Roy Coburn, age 38; (2)Peter McEnay, age 50; (3)Alex Johnson, age 25; (4)Gus Olson (Oleson), age 33, (5)Alfred W. Burns, age 26; (6)Victor Erickson, age 20.

Erickson, who had been entombed in the mine since the fire, was alive when first found by the rescue party, but did not live to reach the surface; his two companions, Otto Johnson and John Fenstrom, were saved. The other five dead men had all been part of the rescue party.

Many of the rescuers were in serious condition from the gases inhaled, but survived. ·The injured included A.A. Bianca, Frank Wurtz, C.A. Waters, W.Z. Kinney, Frank Beers, Dave Lewis, Mike Hennessey and Herman Matson; Matson, near death from exposure to the gases, was hospitalized in Durango and lived the rest of his life in a weakened condition. He continued living in Silverton, working in the mines, died in 1923 at the age of 36 years and is buried at Hillside in an unmarked grave.

The body of 25 year old Alex Johnson was to be shipped to his parents at Ceresco, Nebraska, north of Lincoln. Prosser Undertaking charged his parents $125 plus

$65.20 railway express, a rather high charge for those times. Alex's mother later wrote Mrs. Jessie Kramer in Silverton, saying that the newspaper account of her son's death, sent to her by Mrs. Kramer, gave her more information than anything else she had received. The mother said she had so hoped some of her son's books or keepsakes would be sent to her; however, she received only two telescopes. Alex was a native of Sweden and had worked as a machine man at the Gold King since the previous fall.

Arrangements were made to have the body of Roy Coburn shipped to his parents at Hoisington, Kansas, for which Prosser Undertaking charged a total of $190. Roy had been in Silverton about a year, and had previously worked at Telluride, Ouray and Cripple Creek, Colorado.

Alfred Burns had worked at the Gold Prince Mine before going to work at the Gold King. He was born in Michigan, was a month short of his 27th birthday and had been in the Silverton area about a year; nothing was known of his relatives.

August "Gus" Olson, a native of Sweden, had been in the San Juan country three or four years; he was thought to have a sister at Julesburg, Colorado, a sister at Benson, Nebraska, and a brother at Swedenburg, Nebraska.

Victor Erickson, a native of Finland, was 20 years old and had been working at the Gold King only a couple of months, coming to this area from Old Mexico. Otto Johnson, who was also trapped in the mine but rescued alive, was married to Victor's sister, Hilda. Victor's Finnish name was Karl Viktor Ericksson Gragg.

Mayor John S. Fox issued a proclamation closing all businesses in Silverton on Wednesday, June 10, 1908, and everyone in town attended the funerals or stood along the streets watching. An air of hush and gloom pervaded the little town and everyone in it. That morning the bodies of Roy Coburn and Alex Johnson were put on the train and shipped to their families in Kansas and Nebraska.

The funeral for Peter McEnay was at the Catholic Church in the early afternoon, Rev. Father O'Malley officiating. Many friends attended the sad rites, and at the conclusion, the body was taken to Miners Union Hall where the other three bodies were laid out. The crowd had been gathering long before the hour of the funerals, and many were standing inside and outside the building. Rev. Fred P. Carter, Congregational pastor, conducted the services. Those in the choir were Mrs. Larkin, Delia, George and Alex Bausman, Lew Haas, Art Malchus, John Hughes and David Jones. Many women were in the audience and scores of miners were in attendance to pay their last sad respects to their departed comrades; the main body of the miners formed in rank outside, ready to march to the cemetery. Members of the Elks had seats reserved in the front of the hall, but not nearly all could be accommodated. The four caskets were placed in front of the rostrum; one was purple, official color of the Elks (for Alfred Burns), and the others were somber black. All were covered with beautiful flowers.

"Jesus, Lover of My Soul" was rendered by the choir, then Rev. Carter read from the 23rd Psalm and of resurrection in the 15th chapter of First Corinthians. A duet, "Oh Morning Land" was sung by George Bausman and his sister, Delia. "Their Sun Has Gone Down at Noonday" was the theme of Rev. Carter's funeral sermon, a touching, eloquent and masterly tribute to the brave men who gave up their own lives to save others. The choir then sang "Nearer My God to Thee", after which the large assemblage filed past the open caskets to view the heroic dead.

The procession to the cemetery was the most imposing ever seen in town. More than a thousand men were in line, in addition to a large concourse of carriages. The Firemens' Band played funeral marches and headed the procession; next came the Benevolent and Protective Order of Elks, the Carpenters Union, Industrial Workers of the World, the Junior Band and members of the Silverton Miners Union.

Rev. Carter and Rev. Father O'Malley followed, then the dead men, whose caskets were on wagons. The casket of Alfred Burns was draped with the colors of the Elks, purple and white and the other caskets were draped in black and white. Over all were profusions of flowers. As the long procession slowly wended its way up the hill to the cemetery, the streets on both sides were lined with people contemplating with awe the tragic scene.

When they reached the cemetery, the head of the procession waited at the graves and the lines formed in open order, with uncovered heads, as the caskets were carried to their last resting places. With towering mountains on all sides, the band played "Abide With Me". Rev. Carter then read the burial service of the church, after which came the impressive ritual of the Elks Lodge. The day was beautiful with blue skies and floating white clouds, and the services were very moving. Many tears were shed for the noble spirits of the heroes who gave their lives for their comrades. Burns and Erickson have tombstones at Hillside, McEnay and Olson do not, but are probably buried nearby.

Eleven months later, on the night of May 18, 1909, fire again struck the Gold King property and completely destroyed the newly rebuilt structures. Arthur "The Prince of Wales" Stocks burned to death in those flames and is buried at Hillside in an unmarked grave.


**TOY, LEONARD, JR.** - Son of Leonard, Sr. and Kitty King Toy
(13) - 1911 - Feb 25, 1915 - Age 4 years - His marker was donated in 1993. The angel of death entered the happy home of Leonard and Kitty Toy at Eureka, and bore away the tender soul of their bright little boy. His death was

caused by a sudden and acute attack of tonsillitis. Only the previous week, he and his mother had happily visited friends in Silverton. His death coming so suddenly was indeed a sad, overwhelming and crushing blow to the fond young parents who loved their boy so tenderly. A beautiful child, he already had displayed a natural inherited gift of rare musical talent.

The funeral was held on a Sunday afternoon, and burial was at Hillside. His heartbroken mother never recovered from her little son's death, and died about a year later. She is also buried at Hillside.

*" 'Tis but a little grave, but oh, beware!*
*For world-wide hopes are buried there!*
*And ye, perhaps in coming years,*
*May see, like her, through blinding tears,*
*How much of light, how much of joy,*
*Is buried with that little boy!"*

**TOY, KITTY KING** (Mrs Leonard Toy, Sr.) (13) - Aug 15, 1893 - Jan 24, 1916 - Age 22 Years - Her marker was donated in 1993. On a Sunday morning death claimed as its own the gentle soul of Kitty Toy. She had been ailing for some time, in fact, had never been her former self since the previous February, when her bright little boy died suddenly. Her heart and soul had been wrapped up in her child. The week before Kitty's death Dr. Burnett had performed a very serious operation for cancer, complicated by pregnancy. At first she rallied, but the shock was too great for her system and she worsened, then died.

Born in Johannesburg, South Africa, the daughter of John King and the former Mary Pearce, she had married Leonard Toy at Cardiff, Wales, in 1910. Leonard was visiting in Cornwall, his birthplace, at the time, but he lived in Silverton with his parents, Ben and Mary Moyle Toy. His mother died in Silverton while he was away; her body was returned to her native Cornwall. The newlyweds, Leonard and Kitty, came to America to make their home at Eureka, near Silverton. A 1912 newspaper article described the wonderful Christmas celebration there, at which Kitty Toy played the organ. She was then 19 years old, and her beloved little boy, Leonard, Jr., was about a year old. Just a few short years from the time of that happy Christmas, tragedy and death engulfed them.

*"Christmas Tree at Eureka, Colorado .. This little mountain town was not behind in Christmas festivities! On Monday afternoon you*

would have seen quite a company of young folks going toward the school house, loaded with evergreens and parcels. There, a busy band of workers was decorating the room, while others were at work trimming the large Christmas tree with all kinds of glittering decorations, swinging oranges, apples, packs of candy, and fixing the lights. Needless to say, there was little necessity to ring the bell to call the folks together in the evening, though Master Stanley, the janitor, gave it an extra pull, to ring out merrily. Crowds of children, full of expectancy, trooped along in the glorious silvery light of the welcome moon, which made the grand mountains of near 14,000 feet, with their new coat of brilliant snow, crystallized with frost, glitter like myriads of gems, a sight only to be seen in this wonderful mountain state. The parents were not behind, either, for the school was filled before the time to start, and each brought a suitable gift for the pastor, in the way of some useful household commodity. The school room was a brilliant sight, when the tree was lighted up with the brilliant electric lights.

"The program began by a Christmas carol by the Sunday School, under the leadership of Mrs. Smith. Prayer was offered, another song, then an exercise by the pupils, 'Two little Eyes *to Look to God', followed by solo recitations of Evelyn Gooch, 'Welcome'; by Beatrice Darnell, 'A Christmas Song', recitation by Sarah Jane Casey, a little toddler who did her part well; Helen Gooch recitation 'On Christmas Morning'; Margaret Johnson, solo, 'Long Years Ago'; Maud Stanley, a guitar selection; Blake Casey, a recitation; an action song by the Sunday School; a Christmas hymn by all present; and a five minute talk by the pastor, Rev. J. Bunting Johnson. Mrs. Toy presided at the organ.*

*"After this, the excitement commenced, when Mr. Toelle began to strip the tree of the mysterious packets and to regale all the young folks with candies. The ladies set to work passing around cake and hot coffee to the adults and cake and cocoa to the children. Mr. Casey, of the power company, attended to the lights. The happy assembly came to a close by the Reverend Johnson thanking all who had willingly helped to make the celebration such a success, and by wishing all present, A Very Happy Christmas!"*

Kitty Toy was beloved by all for her nobleness of character, sweet disposition and kindness of heart. Survivors were her husband, Leonard, her mother and two sisters at Cardiff, Wales, a brother in German East Africa, and her father-in-law in Silverton, Benjamin Toy. Kitty was a member of the Eastern Star, under whose auspices the funeral was held. Many friends attended the service, and burial was at Hillside, beside her son.

Kitty's husband, Leonard, was a highly talented musician and played the piano for many musical events in the county. He worked as a mine blacksmith, as his father before him. In 1923 he played at the High School Commencement and as reported in the newspaper, *"His piano solo was a revelation to many Silverton people, his playing being of unusual high order, displaying technique, training and much natural ability"*. He played with a musical group, known as the "Sidney Six", which also included Fenrick Sutherland and Eddie Lorenzon on trumpets, Carl "Sidney" Dillon, violin, Art Lorenzon on drums and Ed "Cheese" Nelson, trombone.

In late August 1916, several months after his young wife's death, Leonard married Mrs. Anna Rosendaal Sitter at Farmington, New Mexico. Both the bride and groom were from Silverton, and they honeymooned at Trimble Springs in the Animas Valley. Children born to them were Douglas and Dowenna. Leonard and his family moved to Jerome, Arizona, in 1926, and he died in San Diego, California, in 1942; his wife, Anna, died in Oakland, California, in 1951.

## TRELOAR, ELIZABETH EVANS

(1) - Oct 17, 1867 - Sept 24, 1902 - Age 34 Years - Her grave is in a fenced enclosure - Elizabeth, a splendid woman, ideal wife and kind mother, died after being ill two weeks. Dr. W.R. Winters, her physician, indicated she died of blood poisoning resulting from an abortion.

Elizabeth was born in Aberystwyth, Cardiganshire, Wales, and came to Silverton in 1896. She and Benjamin Treloar, a well known Cornish miner, were married in Durango on October 17, 1898, and their Silverton friends, Benjamin Dunston and Ellen Andrews, were married at the same time. About a month after the wedding, William and Susan Moyle entertained at a party where Benjamin and Elizabeth were the guests of honor. The newly married couple received many lovely gifts and good wishes. The evening was spent in singing and games, after which bounteous refreshments were served. Ben and Elizabeth later moved to Central City, and had returned to Silverton the previous

July. They were the parents of a son and daughter, James and Edith.

Elizabeth's survivors were her husband, who was foreman at the Silver Lake Mine, and her children, James, three years old, and Edith, age two years. Also two sisters in Silverton, Mrs. Charles E. Jones and Sarah Jane (Mrs. James) Owens; she also had a sister (not named) in Wales. After the funeral service in Silverton, Elizabeth was laid to rest in the Knights of Pythias burying ground at Hillside.

In the spring of 1903, Bennie Treloar took his children, James and Edith, to Redruth, Cornwall, where the children were to live with their grandmother a few years. He returned to Silverton, but eventually moved back to Redruth, remarried and had two more children. He died December 7, 1913, at Redruth, Cornwall.

## ZOSKIE, JOHN SOYKA
No Marker - Died April 13, 1924 - Age 40 Years - John was found dead in a bath tub at the Sunnyside Mine bunkhouse on a Sunday afternoon in April. He had recently been released from Miners Union Hospital after being treated several weeks for severe rheumatism and complications. He planned to

go to Pagosa Springs for the medicinal baths and was advised not to return to work at the mine because of his bad heart.

Coroner Charles Scheer and undertaker Gustav Larson went to Eureka on a railroad motor driven by Nasario Aragon, and the body was brought back to Silverton.

John, referred to as Americanized Polish, was thought to own an unencumbered ranch near Buena Vista. Since he had no near relatives in America, his body was held awaiting word from Buena Vista friends. He was buried at Hillside four days after his death.

*"Life is but a vapor*
*that appears for a moment*
*then vanishes away"*

# EPILOGUE

In July 1884, when Hillside Cemetery was still new (the first burial was in 1875), the *LaPlata Miner* published an unsigned article telling of a visit to the village graveyard. George N. Raymond was the local editor at that time, and J.H. Mountain owned the newspaper. Although there are now many more graves at Hillside, his narrative still perfectly describes the marvelous old graveyard. Those vanished people still invoke the same feelings of curious tenderness from each visitor.

## "OUR VILLAGE GRAVEYARD"
"a place where all things mournful meet,
and yet the sweetest of the sweet,
the stillest of the still"

"We visited one bright sunny day this week our village burying ground. A few lonely graves clustered upon the slope of Boulder Mountain, lying in the path of the morning sun in whose enfolding rays it is wrapped during the day, nor yet deserted by his genial warmth until the last declining rays sink behind the western hill. A pretty sight it is to see at the close of day when the town is already wrapped in shadow, a streak of sunlight still lingering on the spot where lie the departed dead, as if reluctant to desert them, to remove from those few lonely graves its bright sympathy. When even the tops of these high mountains are clothed in the shadows that portend the decline of day, that single ray of light still streams through a cleft in the mountains and lingers there until indeed the day is done and the darkness falls upon the wings of night. On the way we gathered a few of the first wildflowers of the spring with which to decorate some neglected, perhaps forgotten, grave.

"In our city of the dead, undisturbed by the rush and roar of the busy world, silence reigns supreme. All around is hushed and still. No sound disturbs the quiet of the dead, save the breeze sighing through the trees and the roar of the distant rivers and streams.

"From below the sound of the Animas River rushing on its never ceasing journey, tearing over its rocky bed, greeted our ears. In the distance above and around us, on every side, stood the mountains, the eternal hills of God, some with the snows of winter lingering on their tops while, strange coincidence, on their sides below timberline grew the green grass and wildflowers. And aspens, just budding into fresh new life. The sky was blue and fair, the breezes were soft and cooling after our heated climb, and now and then a shy little chipmunk, disturbed on his native and lonely heath, by an intruding and curious stranger, darted across our path, scampering down the hillside at flying speed, and in the solemn firs around and further up the mountain, birds twittered and sang their requiems over the sleeping dead.

"We wandered around through nameless paths between even some nameless graves, lingering with reverence to read the names of those to whose memory some loving hand had erected headstones. A touching sight it was to see, now and then, a name carved out upon a rude board to the memory of some poor soul, perhaps done by a comrade's hand, in whose heart remained a loving remembrance of the dead, yet whose slender purse could not afford the expense of a more fitting monument. Some more fortunate ones, whose friends or relatives are residents of or still linger in the Silver San Juan, have their mounds enclosed in neat fences, and others, still more fortunate, have their virtues carved in marble. Some, alas, perhaps strangers in a strange land, have nothing but a mass of rocks and an uninscribed board at the foot and head, to point out to the passerby a grave. Only a stranger's grave, a grass-grown grave, no carved stone tells who is lying here. No flowers upon this mound are strewn. Upon it falls no tear. Loving hands had placed upon one grave and wreathed around the headstone, a branch or two of fragrant fir and planted the sweet wild rose.

"From the babe to the person crowned with the weight of years, all lie buried here. Youth and age, together sleeping their long sleep, undisturbed by the trials and perplexities of life. Beside whose graves, in silence and alone, removed from the haunts of men, one can forget the petty grievances of the earth. Look from nature up to nature's God. And listen to far more eloquent appeals from each grave, each tiny mound, than were ever preached by the tongue of man.

"A holy quietude is here, save for the happy birdling song which breaks through the stillness, pure and clear, and echoes the dark firs among."

Also available from

113 Hal freda28@juno.com<br>Freda Peterson Gooch<br>804 Empire, Box 610<br>Silverton, CO 81433 73069

**The Obstinate Land**
   by Harold Keith: $12.95 paper

**Will Rogers, A Boy's Life**
   by Harold Keith: $17.00 hard; $11.00 paper

**Komantcia**
   by Harold Keith: $17.00 hard

**The Sound of Strings**
   by Harold Keith: $17.00 hard

**Philippines Defender: A Fighter Pilot's Diary**
   by David Obert: $12.95 paper

**By George! For Lilly/Love Letters**
   **to a Potbellied Stove**
   by George Levite: $11.95 paper

**Sooner Said And Done**
   by Ed Montgomery: $25.00 hard; $9.00 paper

**They Carried The Torch**
   by Elva Ferguson: $5.00 paper

**The Remarkable Ride of the Abernathy Boys**
   by Robert B. Jackson: $6.00 paper

Shipping:  $2.00 for first book,
           $1.00 for each additional book